Overla

Party ... oat requesting redress; a boat ... 69.1; a race committee or an o...).

Postpo ... duled start but may be started

Proper Course A course a boat would sail to *finish* as soon as possible in the absence of the other boats referred to in the rule using the term. A boat has no *proper course* before her starting signal.

Protest An allegation made under rule 61.2 by a boat, a race committee or a protest committee that a boat has broken a *rule*.

Racing A boat is *racing* from her preparatory signal until she *finishes* and clears the finishing line and *marks* or retires, or until the race committee signals a general recall, *postponement* or *abandonment*.

Room The space a boat needs in the existing conditions while manoeuvring promptly in a seamanlike way.

Rule
(a) The rules in this book, including the Definitions, Race Signals, Introduction, preambles and the rules of relevant appendices, but not titles;

(b) ISAF Regulation 19, Eligibility Code; Regulation 20, Advertising Code; and Regulation 21, Anti-Doping Code;

(c) the prescriptions of the national authority, unless they are changed by the sailing instructions in compliance with the national authority's prescription, if any, to rule 87;

(d) the class rules (for a boat racing under a handicap or rating system, the rules of that system are 'class rules');

(e) the notice of race;

(f) the sailing instructions; and

(g) any other documents that govern the event.

Start A boat *starts* when, having been entirely on the pre-start side of the starting line at or after her starting signal, and having complied with rule 30.1 if it applies, any part of her hull, crew or equipment crosses the starting line in the direction of the first *mark*.

Tack, Starboard or Port A boat is on the *tack, starboard* or *port*, corresponding to her *windward* side.

Two-Length Zone The area around a *mark* or *obstruction* within a distance of two hull lengths of the boat nearer to it.

Windward See **Leeward and Windward**.

RACING CHARTER

Objectives

- To provide the framework for everyone to enjoy the sport of sailboat racing in whatever capacity and to whatever level the individual desires.
- To ensure that the sport of sailboat racing welcomes people and treats them equally.
- To ensure that those who experience sailboat racing are encouraged to continue.

Principles and Practices

- The sport welcomes all participants; it relies largely on self-compliance and self-policing. Those that deliberately take unfair advantage of this or behave in an inappropriate manner, either on or off the water, can expect to be brought to account.
- Competitors agree to compete and behave in compliance with the rules and in accordance with accepted standards of sailboat racing. When involved in a genuine dispute, both the parties to the dispute and those deciding the matter will use the established procedures for achieving resolution.
- Foul or abusive language, intimidation, aggressive behaviour or lack of respect for others and their property will not be tolerated.
- Organizers, officials and other providers of sailboat racing agree to strive to provide the fairest racing possible. This includes encouraging feed-back and facilitating the resolution of genuine disputes (including protests) in a timely and proper manner.
- Coaches and other advisors agree to encourage their charges to compete, officiate or behave only in compliance with the above principles and practices.

This Charter applies equally to those who organize, manage, coach, advise, judge, provide services and compete (including those who support competitors) in sailboat racing.

The RYA encourages the adoption and implementation of this Charter, and provides guidance and support to individuals and organizations to assist implementation. This guidance and support is consistent with any practices of the International Sailing Federation.

For further information visit www.rya.org.uk/racing/charter

APPLICATION OF RYA RACING CHARTER

Through its Racing Charter, the RYA seeks to promote fair and enjoyable racing for all.

Competitors who sail under the Charter should expect:

- to be provided with racing that, as far as is possible, is fair, enjoyable and safe;
- to receive services that conform to those guidelines endorsed by the RYA and appropriate to the event;
- to be able to inform Organizing Authorities when any racing services are not provided to acceptable standards;
- to be provided with prompt services to resolve any disputes.

Competitors who sail under the Charter are expected:

- to show courtesy and respect to other competitors and officials, and to other users of the water;
- to compete in compliance with the rules, and take a penalty when required by the rules;
- to use the provided services to resolve any disputes.

Expectations of Clubs that organize racing under the Charter may be found at www.rya.org.uk/racing/charter

Rule 69 is used by the sport of sailboat racing to control and penalize unacceptable behaviour at an event. Guidelines on its application in the UK are included on page 169 of this rule book.

The RACING RULES of SAILING

for 2005–2008

Including the RYA Prescriptions

Royal Yachting Association
RYA House, Ensign Way, Hamble
Southampton SO41 4YA
Tel: 0845 345 0400
Fax: 0845 345 0329
E-mail: admin@rya.org.uk
Web site: www.rya.org.uk

© International Sailing Federation, (IOM) Ltd.
June 2004

Published by the Royal Yachting Association
RYA website: www.rya.org.uk
© Royal Yachting Association, October 2004

CONTENTS

INTRODUCTION

The Racing Rules of Sailing includes two main sections. The first, Parts 1–7, contains rules that affect all competitors. The second, Appendices A–P, provides details of rules, rules that apply to particular kinds of racing, and rules that affect only a small number of competitors or officials.

Revision The racing rules are revised and published every four years by the International Sailing Federation (ISAF), the international authority for the sport. This edition becomes effective on 1 January 2005. Marginal markings indicate important changes to Parts 1–7 and the Definitions of the 2001–2004 edition. No changes are contemplated before 2009, but any changes determined to be urgent before then will be announced through national authorities and posted on the ISAF website (www.sailing.org).

ISAF Codes The ISAF Eligibility, Advertising and Anti-Doping Codes (Regulations 19, 20 and 21) are referred to in the definition *Rule* but they can be changed at any time. Regulations 19 and 20 are included in this book on blue coloured pages. New versions will be announced through national authorities and posted on the ISAF website.

Cases and Calls The ISAF publishes interpretations of the racing rules in *The Case Book for 2005–2008* and recognizes them as authoritative interpretations and explanations of the rules. It also publishes *The Call Book for Match Racing for 2005–2008* and *The Call Book for Team Racing for 2005–2008*, and it recognizes them as authoritative only for umpired match or team racing. These publications are available on the ISAF website.

Terminology A term used in the sense stated in the Definitions is printed in italics or, in preambles, in bold italics (for example, *racing* and ***racing***). 'Boat' means a sailboat and the crew on board. 'Race committee' includes any person or committee performing a race committee function. Other words and terms are used in the sense ordinarily understood in nautical or general use.

Appendices When the rules of an appendix apply, they take precedence over any conflicting rules in Parts 1–7. Each appendix is identified by a letter. A reference to a rule in an appendix will contain the letter and the rule number (for example, 'rule A1'). There is no Appendix I or O.

Changes to the Rules The prescriptions of a national authority, class rules or the sailing instructions may change a racing rule only as permitted in rule 86.

RYA Prescriptions to the racing rules are on yellow pages 163-167. A rule with a prescription is marked with a RYA logo (**RYA**) in the margin. The RYA prescriptions may be changed only as stated in the prescription to rule 87.

The **RYA** will announce changes to the rules and ISAF codes and will publish any changes to the RYA prescriptions on the RYA website (www.rya.org.uk/racing/rules.asp).

BASIC PRINCIPLE

SPORTSMANSHIP AND THE RULES

Competitors in the sport of sailing are governed by a body of *rules* that they are expected to follow and enforce. A fundamental principle of sportsmanship is that when competitors break a *rule* they will promptly take a penalty, which may be to retire.

PART 1 - FUNDAMENTAL RULES

1 SAFETY

1.1 Helping Those in Danger

A boat or competitor shall give all possible help to any person or vessel in danger.

1.2 Life-Saving Equipment and Personal Buoyancy

A boat shall carry adequate life-saving equipment for all persons on board, including one item ready for immediate use, unless her class rules make some other provision. Each competitor is individually responsible for wearing personal buoyancy adequate for the conditions.

2 FAIR SAILING

A boat and her owner shall compete in compliance with recognized principles of sportsmanship and fair play. A boat may be penalized under this rule only if it is clearly established that these principles have been violated. A disqualification under this rule shall not be excluded from the boat's series score.

3 ACCEPTANCE OF THE RULES

By participating in a race conducted under these racing rules, each competitor and boat owner agrees

(a) to be governed by the *rules;*

(b) to accept the penalties imposed and other action taken under the *rules,* subject to the appeal and review procedures provided in them, as the final determination of any matter arising under the *rules*; and

(c) with respect to such determination, not to resort to any court or other tribunal not provided by the *rules*.

4 DECISION TO RACE

The responsibility for a boat's decision to participate in a race or to continue *racing* is hers alone.

5 BANNED SUBSTANCES AND METHODS

A competitor shall neither take a substance nor use a method banned by the Olympic Movement Anti-Doping Code or the World Anti-Doping Agency and shall comply with ISAF Regulation 21, Anti-Doping Code. An alleged or actual breach of this rule shall be dealt with under Regulation 21. It shall not be grounds for a *protest* and rule 63.1 does not apply.

PART 2 - WHEN BOATS MEET

The rules of Part 2 apply between boats that are sailing in or near the racing area and intend to **race**, *are* **racing**, *or have been* **racing**. *However, a boat not* **racing** *shall not be penalized for breaking one of these rules, except rule 22.1. When a boat sailing under these rules meets a vessel that is not, she shall comply with the* International Regulations for Preventing Collisions at Sea (IRPCAS) *or government right-of-way rules. However, an alleged breach of those rules shall not be grounds for a* **protest** *except by the race committee or protest committee. If the sailing instructions so state, the rules of Part 2 are replaced by the right-of-way rules of the* IRPCAS *or by government right-of-way rules.*

Section A - Right of Way

A boat has right of way when another boat is required to **keep clear** *of her. However, some rules in Sections B, C and D limit the actions of a right-of-way boat.*

10 ON OPPOSITE TACKS

When boats are on opposite *tacks*, a *port-tack* boat shall *keep clear* of a *starboard-tack* boat.

11 ON THE SAME TACK, OVERLAPPED

When boats are on the same *tack* and *overlapped*, a *windward* boat shall *keep clear* of a *leeward* boat.

12 ON THE SAME TACK, NOT OVERLAPPED

When boats are on the same *tack* and not *overlapped*, a boat *clear astern* shall *keep clear* of a boat *clear ahead*.

13 WHILE TACKING

After a boat passes head to wind, she shall *keep clear* of other boats until she is on a close-hauled course. During that time rules 10, 11 and 12 do not apply. If two boats are subject to this rule at the same time, the one on the other's port side or the one astern shall *keep clear*.

Section B - General Limitations

14 AVOIDING CONTACT

A boat shall avoid contact with another boat if reasonably possible. However, a right-of-way boat or one entitled to *room*

(a) need not act to avoid contact until it is clear that the other boat is not *keeping clear* or giving *room*, and

(b) shall not be penalized under this rule unless there is contact that causes damage or injury.

15 ACQUIRING RIGHT OF WAY

When a boat acquires right of way, she shall initially give the other boat *room* to *keep clear*, unless she acquires right of way because of the other boat's actions.

16 CHANGING COURSE

16.1 When a right-of-way boat changes course, she shall give the other boat *room* to *keep clear*.

16.2 In addition, when after the starting signal a *port-tack* boat is *keeping clear* by sailing to pass astern of a *starboard-tack* boat, the *starboard-tack* boat shall not change course if as a result the *port-tack* boat would immediately need to change course to continue *keeping clear*.

17 ON THE SAME TACK; PROPER COURSE

17.1 If a boat *clear astern* becomes *overlapped* within two of her hull lengths to *leeward* of a boat on the same *tack*, she shall not sail above her *proper course* while they remain *overlapped* within that distance, unless in doing so she promptly sails astern of the other boat. This rule does not apply if the *overlap* begins while the *windward* boat is required by rule 13 to *keep clear*.

17.2 Except on a beat to windward, while a boat is less than two of her hull lengths from a *leeward* boat or a boat *clear astern* steering a course to *leeward* of her, she shall not sail below her *proper course* unless she gybes.

Section C - At Marks and Obstructions

To the extent that a Section C rule conflicts with a rule in Section A or B, the Section C rule takes precedence.

18 ROUNDING AND PASSING MARKS AND OBSTRUCTIONS

*In rule 18, **room** is **room** for an inside boat to round or pass between an outside boat and a **mark** or **obstruction**, including **room** to tack or gybe when either is a normal part of the manoeuvre.*

18.1 When This Rule Applies

Rule 18 applies when boats are about to round or pass a *mark* they are required to leave on the same side, or an *obstruction* on the same side, until they have passed it. However, it does not apply

(a) at a starting *mark* surrounded by navigable water or at its anchor line from the time the boats are approaching them to *start* until they have passed them, or

(b) while the boats are on opposite *tacks*, either on a beat to windward or when the *proper course* for one of them, but not both, to round or pass the *mark* or *obstruction* is to tack.

18.2 Giving Room; Keeping Clear

(a) OVERLAPPED - BASIC RULE

When boats are *overlapped* the outside boat shall give the inside boat *room* to round or pass the *mark* or *obstruction*, and if the inside boat has right of way the outside boat shall also *keep clear*. Other parts of rule 18 contain exceptions to this rule.

(b) OVERLAPPED AT THE ZONE

If boats were *overlapped* before either of them reached the *two-length zone* and the *overlap* is broken after one of them has reached it, the boat that was on the outside shall continue to give the other boat *room*. If the outside boat becomes *clear astern* or *overlapped* inside the other boat, she is not entitled to *room* and shall *keep clear*.

(c) NOT OVERLAPPED AT THE ZONE

If a boat was clear ahead at the time she reached the *two-length zone*, the boat *clear astern* shall thereafter *keep clear*. If the boat *clear astern* becomes *overlapped* outside the other boat, she shall also give the inside boat *room*. If the boat *clear astern* becomes *overlapped* inside the other boat, she is not entitled to *room*. If the boat that was *clear ahead* passes head to wind, rule 18.2(c) no longer applies and remains inapplicable.

(d) CHANGING COURSE TO ROUND OR PASS

When after the starting signal rule 18 applies between two boats and the right-of-way boat is changing course to round or pass a *mark*, rule 16 does not apply between her and the other boat.

(e) OVERLAP RIGHTS

If there is reasonable doubt that a boat obtained or broke an *overlap* in time, it shall be presumed that she did not. If the outside boat is unable to give *room* when an *overlap* begins, rules 18.2(a) and 18.2(b) do not apply.

18.3 Tacking at a Mark

If two boats were approaching a *mark* on opposite *tacks* and one of them completes a tack in the *two-length zone* when the other is fetching the *mark*, rule 18.2 does not apply. The boat that tacked

(a) shall not cause the other boat to sail above close-hauled to avoid her or prevent the other boat from passing the *mark*, and

(b) shall give *room* if the other boat becomes *overlapped* inside her, in which case rule 15 does not apply.

18.4 Gybing

When an inside *overlapped* right-of-way boat must gybe at a *mark* or *obstruction* to sail her *proper course*, until she gybes she shall sail no farther from the *mark* or *obstruction* than needed to sail that course.

18.5 Passing a Continuing Obstruction

While boats are passing a continuing *obstruction*, rules 18.2(b) and 18.2(c) do not apply. A boat *clear astern* that obtains an inside *overlap* is entitled to *room* to pass between the other boat and the *obstruction* only if at the moment the *overlap* begins there is *room* to do so. If there is not, she is not entitled to *room* and shall *keep clear.*

19 ROOM TO TACK AT AN OBSTRUCTION

19.1 When approaching an *obstruction*, a boat sailing close-hauled or above may hail for *room* to tack and avoid another boat on the same *tack*. However, she shall not hail unless safety requires her to make a substantial course change to avoid the *obstruction*. Before tacking she shall give the hailed boat time to respond. The hailed boat shall respond by either

(a) tacking as soon as possible, in which case the hailing boat shall also tack as soon as possible, or

(b) immediately replying "You tack", in which case the hailing boat shall tack as soon as possible and the hailed boat shall give *room*, and rules 10 and 13 do not apply.

19.2 Rule 19.1 does not apply at a starting *mark* surrounded by navigable water or at its anchor line from the time boats are approaching them to *start* until they have passed them or at a *mark* that the hailed boat can fetch. When rule 19.1 applies, rule 18 does not.

Section D - Other Rules

When rule 20 or 21 applies between two boats, Section A rules do not.

20 STARTING ERRORS; PENALTY TURNS; MOVING ASTERN

20.1 A boat sailing towards the pre-start side of the starting line or its extensions after her starting signal to *start* or to comply with rule 30.1 shall *keep clear* of a boat not doing so until she is completely on the pre-start side.

20.2 A boat making a penalty turn shall *keep clear* of one that is not.

20.3 A boat moving astern by backing a sail shall *keep clear* of one that is not.

21 CAPSIZED, ANCHORED OR AGROUND; RESCUING

If possible, a boat shall avoid a boat that is capsized or has not regained control after capsizing, is anchored or aground, or is trying to help a person or vessel in danger. A boat is capsized when her masthead is in the water.

22 INTERFERING WITH ANOTHER BOAT

22.1 If reasonably possible, a boat not *racing* shall not interfere with a boat that is *racing*.

22.2 A boat shall not change course if her only purpose is to interfere with a boat making a penalty turn or one on another leg or lap of the course.

PART 3 - CONDUCT OF A RACE

25 NOTICE OF RACE, SAILING INSTRUCTIONS AND SIGNALS

The notice of race and sailing instructions shall be made available to each boat before a race begins. The meanings of the visual and sound signals stated in Race Signals shall not be changed except under rule 86.1(b). The meanings of any other signals that may be used shall be stated in the sailing instructions.

26 STARTING RACES

Races shall be started by using the following signals. Times shall be taken from the visual signals; the absence of a sound signal shall be disregarded.

Signal	*Flag*	*Sound*	*Minutes before starting signal*
Warning	Class flag	1 sound	5*
Preparatory	P, I, Z, Z with I, or black flag	1 sound	4
One-minute	Preparatory flag removed	1 long sound	1
Starting	Class flag removed	1 sound	0

* or as stated in the sailing instructions

The warning signal for each succeeding class shall be made with or after the starting signal of the preceding class.

27 OTHER RACE COMMITTEE ACTIONS BEFORE THE STARTING SIGNAL

27.1 No later than the warning signal, the race committee shall signal or otherwise designate the course to be sailed if the sailing instructions have not stated the course, and it may replace one course signal with another and signal that wearing personal buoyancy is required (display flag Y with one sound).

27.2 No later than the preparatory signal, the race committee may move a starting *mark* and may apply rule 30.

27.3 Before the starting signal, the race committee may for any reason *postpone* (display flag AP, AP over H, or AP over A, with two sounds) or *abandon* the race (display flag N over H, or N over A, with three sounds).

28 SAILING THE COURSE

28.1 A boat shall *start*, leave each *mark* on the required side in the correct order, and *finish*, so that a string representing her wake after *starting* and until *finishing* would when drawn taut pass each *mark* on the required side and touch each rounding *mark*. She may correct any errors to comply with this rule. After *finishing* she need not cross the finishing line completely.

28.2 A boat may leave on either side a *mark* that does not begin, bound or end the leg she is on. However, she shall leave a starting *mark* on the required side when she is approaching the starting line from its pre-start side to *start*.

29 RECALLS

29.1 Individual Recall

When at a boat's starting signal any part of her hull, crew or equipment is on the course side of the starting line or she must comply with rule 30.1, the race committee shall promptly display flag X with one sound. The flag shall be displayed until all such boats are completely on the pre-start side of the starting line or its extensions and have complied with rule 30.1 if it applies, but not later than four minutes after the starting signal or one minute before any later starting signal, whichever is earlier.

29.2 General Recall

When at the starting signal the race committee is unable to identify boats that are on the course side of the starting line or to which rule 30 applies, or there has been an error in the starting procedure, the race committee may signal a general recall (display the First Substitute with two sounds). The warning signal for a new start for the recalled class shall be made one minute after the First Substitute is removed (one sound), and the starts for any succeeding classes shall follow the new start.

30 STARTING PENALTIES

30.1 Round-an-End Rule

If flag I has been displayed, and any part of a boat's hull, crew or equipment is on the course side of the starting line or its extensions during the minute before her starting signal, she shall thereafter sail from the course side across an extension to the pre-start side before *starting*.

30.2 20% Penalty Rule

If flag Z has been displayed, no part of a boat's hull, crew or equipment shall be in the triangle formed by the ends of the starting line and the first *mark* during the minute before her starting signal. If a boat breaks this rule and is identified, she shall receive, without a hearing, a 20% scoring penalty calculated as stated in rule 44.3(c). She shall be penalized even if the race is restarted, resailed or rescheduled, but not if it is *postponed* or *abandoned* before the starting signal.

30.3 Black Flag Rule

If a black flag has been displayed, no part of a boat's hull, crew or equipment shall be in the triangle formed by the ends of the starting line and the first *mark* during the minute before her starting signal. If a boat breaks this rule and is identified, she shall be disqualified without a hearing, even if the race is restarted, resailed or rescheduled, but not if it is *postponed* or *abandoned* before the starting signal. If a general recall is signalled or the race is *abandoned* after the starting signal, the race committee shall display her sail number before the next warning signal for that race, and if the race is restarted or resailed she shall not sail in it. If she does so, her disqualification shall not be excluded in calculating her series score. If this rule applies rule 29.1 does not.

31 TOUCHING A MARK

31.1 While *racing*, a boat shall not touch a starting *mark* before starting, a *mark* that begins, bounds or ends the leg of the course on which she is sailing, or a finishing *mark* after *finishing*.

31.2 A boat that has broken rule 31.1 may, after getting well clear of other boats as soon as possible, take a penalty by promptly making one turn including one tack and one gybe. When a boat takes the penalty after touching a finishing *mark*, she shall sail completely to the course side of the line before *finishing*. However, if a boat has gained a significant advantage in the race or series by touching the *mark* her penalty shall be to retire.

32 SHORTENING OR ABANDONING AFTER THE START

32.1 After the starting signal, the race committee may shorten the course (display flag S with two sounds) or *abandon* the race (display flag N, N over H, or N over A, with three sounds), as appropriate,

(a) because of an error in the starting procedure,

(b) because of foul weather,

(c) because of insufficient wind making it unlikely that any boat will *finish* within the time limit,

(d) because a *mark* is missing or out of position, or

(e) for any other reason directly affecting the safety or fairness of the competition,

or may shorten the course so that other scheduled races can be sailed. However, after one boat has sailed the course and *finished* within the time limit, if any, the race committee shall not *abandon* the race without considering the consequences for all boats in the race or series.

32.2 If the race committee signals a shortened course (displays flag S with two sounds), the finishing line shall be,

(a) at a rounding *mark*, between the *mark* and a staff displaying flag S;

(b) at a line boats are required to cross at the end of each lap, that line;

(c) at a gate, between the gate *marks*.

33 CHANGING THE NEXT LEG OF THE COURSE

The race committee may change a leg of the course that begins at a rounding mark by changing the position of the next *mark* (or the finishing line) and signalling all boats before they begin the leg. The next *mark* need not be in position at that time.

(a) If the direction of the leg will be changed, the signal shall be the display of flag C with repetitive sounds and either

(1) the new compass bearing or

(2) a green triangular flag or board for a change to starboard or a red rectangular flag or board for a change to port.

(b) If the length of the leg will be changed, the signal shall be the display of flag C with repetitive sounds and a '–' if the leg will be shortened or a '+' if the leg will be lengthened.

(a) Subsequent legs may be changed without further signalling to maintain the course shape.

34 MARK MISSING

If a *mark* is missing or out of position, the race committee shall, if possible,

(a) replace it in its correct position or substitute a new one of similar appearance, or

(b) substitute an object displaying flag M and make repetitive sound signals.

35 TIME LIMIT AND SCORES

If one boat sails the course as required by rule 28.1 and *finishes* within the time limit, if any, all boats that *finish* shall be scored according to their finishing places unless the race is *abandoned*. If no boat *finishes* within the time limit, the race committee shall *abandon* the race.

36 RACES TO BE RESTARTED OR RESAILED

If a race is restarted or resailed, a breach of a *rule*, other than rule 30.3, in the original race shall not prohibit a boat from competing or, except under rule 30.2, 30.3 or 69, cause her to be penalized.

PART 4 - OTHER REQUIREMENTS WHEN RACING

Part 4 rules apply only to boats ***racing****.*

40 PERSONAL BUOYANCY; HARNESSES

40.1 When flag Y is displayed with one sound before or with the warning signal, competitors shall wear life-jackets or other adequate personal buoyancy. Wet suits and dry suits are not adequate personal buoyancy.

40.2 A trapeze or hiking harness shall have a device that can quickly release the competitor from the boat at any time while in use.

Note: This rule takes effect on 1 January 2006

41 OUTSIDE HELP

A boat shall not receive help from any outside source, except

(a) help as provided for in rule 1;

(b) help for an ill or injured crew member;

(c) after a collision, help from the crew of the other boat to get clear;

(d) help in the form of information freely available to all boats;

(e) unsolicited information from a disinterested source, which may be another boat in the same race.

42 PROPULSION

42.1 Basic Rule

Except when permitted in rule 42.3 or 45, a boat shall compete by using only the wind and water to increase, maintain or decrease her speed. Her crew may adjust the trim of sails and hull, and perform other acts of seamanship, but shall not otherwise move their bodies to propel the boat.

42.2 Prohibited Actions

Without limiting the application of rule 42.1, these actions are prohibited:

(a) pumping: repeated fanning of any sail either by pulling in and releasing the sail or by vertical or athwartships body movement;

(b) rocking: repeated rolling of the boat, induced by

(1) body movement,

(2) repeated adjustment of the sails or centreboard, or

(3) steering;

(c) ooching: sudden forward body movement, stopped abruptly;

(d) sculling: repeated movement of the helm that is either forceful or that propels the boat forward or prevents her from moving astern;

(e) repeated tacks or gybes unrelated to changes in the wind or to tactical considerations.

42.3 Exceptions

(a) A boat may be rolled to facilitate steering.

(b) A boat's crew may move their bodies to exaggerate the rolling that facilitates steering the boat through a tack or a gybe, provided that, just after the tack or gybe is completed, the boat's speed is not greater than it would have been in the absence of the tack or gybe.

(c) Except on a beat to windward, when surfing (rapidly accelerating down the leeward side of a wave) or planing is possible, the boat's crew may pull the sheet and the guy controlling any sail in order to initiate surfing or planing, but only once for each wave or gust of wind.

(d) When a boat is above a close-hauled course and either stationary or moving slowly, she may scull to turn to a close-hauled course.

(e) A boat may reduce speed by repeatedly moving her helm.

(f) Any means of propulsion may be used to help a person or another vessel in danger.

(g) To get clear after grounding or colliding with another boat or object, a boat may use force applied by the crew of either boat and any equipment other than a propulsion engine.

Note: Interpretations of rule 42 are available at the ISAF website (www.sailing.org) or by mail upon request.

43 COMPETITOR CLOTHING AND EQUIPMENT

43.1 (a) Competitors shall not wear or carry clothing or equipment for the purpose of increasing their weight.

(b) Furthermore, a competitor's clothing and equipment shall not weigh more than 8 kilograms, excluding a hiking or trapeze harness and clothing (including footwear) worn only below the knee. Class rules or sailing instructions may specify a lower weight or a higher weight up to 10 kilograms. Class rules may include footwear and other clothing worn below the knee within that weight. A hiking or trapeze harness shall have positive buoyancy and shall not weigh more than 2 kilograms, except that class rules may specify a higher weight up to 4 kilograms. Weights shall be determined as required by Appendix H.

(c) When a measurer in charge of weighing clothing and equipment believes a competitor may have broken rule 43.1(a) or 43.1(b) he shall report the matter in writing to the race committee, which shall protest the boat of the competitor.

43.2 Rule 43.1(b) does not apply to boats required to be equipped with lifelines.

44 PENALTIES FOR BREAKING RULES OF PART 2

44.1 Taking a Penalty

A boat that may have broken a rule of Part 2 while *racing* may take a penalty at the time of the incident. Her penalty shall be a Two-Turns Penalty unless the sailing instructions specify the use of the

Scoring Penalty or some other penalty. However, if she caused injury or serious damage or gained a significant advantage in the race or series by her breach her penalty shall be to retire.

44.2 **Two-Turns Penalty**

After getting well clear of other boats as soon after the incident as possible, a boat takes a Two-Turns Penalty by promptly making two turns in the same direction, including two tacks and two gybes. When a boat takes the penalty at or near the finishing line, she shall sail completely to the course side of the line before *finishing*.

44.3 **Scoring Penalty**

(a) A boat takes a Scoring Penalty by displaying a yellow flag at the first reasonable opportunity after the incident, keeping it displayed until *finishing*, and calling the race committee's attention to it at the finishing line. At that time she shall also inform the race committee of the identity of the other boat involved in the incident. If this is impracticable, she shall do so at the first reasonable opportunity within the time limit for *protests*.

(b) If a boat displays a yellow flag, she shall also comply with the other parts of rule 44.3(a).

(c) The boat's penalty score shall be the score for the place worse than her actual finishing place by the number of places stated in the sailing instructions, except that she shall not be scored worse than Did Not Finish. When the sailing instructions do not state the number of places, the number shall be the whole number (rounding 0.5 upward) nearest to 20% of the number of boats entered. The scores of other boats shall not be changed; therefore, two boats may receive the same score.

44.4 **Limits on Penalties**

(a) When a boat intends to take a penalty as provided in rule 44.1 and in the same incident has touched a *mark*, she need not take the penalty provided in rule 31.2.

(b) A boat that takes a penalty shall not be penalized further with respect to the same incident unless she failed to retire when rule 44.1 required her to do so.

45 HAULING OUT; MAKING FAST; ANCHORING

A boat shall be afloat and off moorings at her preparatory signal. Thereafter, she shall not be hauled out or made fast except to bail out, reef sails or make repairs. She may anchor or the crew may stand on the bottom. She shall recover the anchor before continuing in the race unless she is unable to do so.

46 PERSON IN CHARGE

A boat shall have on board a person in charge designated by the member or organization that entered the boat. See rule 75.

47 LIMITATIONS ON EQUIPMENT AND CREW

47.1 A boat shall use only the equipment on board at her preparatory signal.

47.2 No person on board shall intentionally leave, except when ill or injured, or to help a person or vessel in danger, or to swim. A person leaving the boat by accident or to swim shall be back on board before the boat continues in the race.

48 FOG SIGNALS AND LIGHTS

When safety requires, a boat shall sound fog signals and show lights as required by the *International Regulations for Preventing Collisions at Sea* or applicable government rules.

49 CREW POSITION

49.1 Competitors shall use no device designed to position their bodies outboard, other than hiking straps and stiffeners worn under the thighs.

49.2 When lifelines are required by the class rules or the sailing instructions they shall be taut, and competitors shall not position any part of their torsos outside them, except briefly to perform a necessary task. On boats equipped with upper and lower lifelines of wire, a competitor sitting on the deck facing outboard with his waist inside the lower lifeline may have the upper part of his body outside the upper lifeline.

50 SETTING AND SHEETING SAILS

50.1 Changing Sails

When headsails or spinnakers are being changed, a replacing sail may be fully set and trimmed before the replaced sail is lowered. However, only one mainsail and, except when changing, only one spinnaker shall be carried set at a time.

50.2 Spinnaker Poles, Whisker Poles

Only one spinnaker pole or whisker pole shall be used at a time except when gybing. When in use, it shall be attached to the foremost mast.

50.3 Use of Outriggers

(a) No sail shall be sheeted over or through an outrigger, except as permitted in rule 50.3(b) or 50.3(c). An outrigger is any fitting or other device so placed that it could exert outward pressure on a sheet or sail at a point from which, with the boat upright, a vertical line would fall outside the hull or deck planking. For the purpose of this rule, bulwarks, rails and rubbing strakes are not part of the hull or deck planking and the following are not outriggers: a bowsprit used to secure the tack of a working sail, a bumkin used to sheet the boom of a working sail, or a boom of a boomed headsail that requires no adjustment when tacking.

(b) Any sail may be sheeted to or led above a boom that is regularly used for a working sail and is permanently attached to the mast from which the head of the working sail is set.

(c) A headsail may be sheeted or attached at its clew to a spinnaker pole or whisker pole, provided that a spinnaker is not set.

RYA 50.4 **Headsails**

The difference between a headsail and a spinnaker is that the mid-girth of a headsail, measured from the mid-points of its luff and leech, does not exceed 50% of the length of its foot, and no other intermediate girth exceeds a percentage similarly proportional to its distance from the head of the sail. A sail tacked down behind the foremost mast is not a headsail.

51 MOVABLE BALLAST

All movable ballast shall be properly stowed, and water, dead weight or ballast shall not be moved for the purpose of changing trim or stability. Floorboards, bulkheads, doors, stairs and water tanks shall be left in place and all cabin fixtures kept on board.

52 MANUAL POWER

A boat's standing rigging, running rigging, spars and movable hull appendages shall be adjusted and operated only by manual power.

53 SKIN FRICTION

A boat shall not eject or release a substance, such as a polymer, or have specially textured surfaces that could improve the character of the flow of water inside the boundary layer.

54 FORESTAYS AND HEADSAIL TACKS

Forestays and headsail tacks, except those of spinnaker staysails when the boat is not close-hauled, shall be attached approximately on a boat's centreline.

PART 5
PROTESTS, REDRESS, HEARINGS, MISCONDUCT AND APPEALS

Section A - **Protests; Redress; Rule 69 Action**

60 RIGHT TO PROTEST; RIGHT TO REQUEST REDRESS OR RULE 69 ACTION

60.1 A boat may

(a) protest another boat, but not for an alleged breach of a rule of Part 2 unless she was involved in or saw the incident; or

(b) request redress.

60.2 A race committee may

(a) protest a boat, but not as a result of a report from an *interested party* or information in an invalid *protest* or in a request for redress;

(b) request redress for a boat; or

(c) report to the protest committee requesting action under rule 69.1(a).

60.3 A protest committee may

(a) protest a boat, but not as a result of a report from an *interested party* or information in an invalid *protest* or in a request for redress. However, it may protest a boat

(1) if it learns of an incident involving her that may have resulted in injury or serious damage, or

(2) if during the hearing of a valid *protest* it learns that the boat, although not a *party* to the hearing, was involved in the incident and may have broken a *rule;*

(b) call a hearing to consider redress; or

(c) act under rule 69.1(a).

61 PROTEST REQUIREMENTS

61.1 Informing the Protestee

(a) A boat intending to protest shall inform the other boat at the first reasonable opportunity. When her *protest* concerns an incident in the racing area that she is involved in or sees, she shall hail 'Protest' and conspicuously display a red flag at the first reasonable opportunity for each. She shall display the flag until she is no longer *racing*. However,

(1) if the other boat is beyond hailing distance, the protesting boat need not hail but she shall inform the other boat at the first reasonable opportunity;

(2) if the hull length of the protesting boat is less than 6 metres, she need not display a red flag;

(3) if the incident results in damage or injury that is obvious to the boats involved and one of them intends to protest, the requirements of this rule do not apply to her, but she shall attempt to inform the other boat within the time limit of rule 61.3.

(b) A race committee or protest committee intending to protest a boat shall inform her as soon as reasonably possible. However, if the *protest* arises from an incident the committee observes in the racing area, it shall inform the boat after the race within the time limit of rule 61.3.

(c) If the protest committee decides to protest a boat under rule 60.3(a)(2), it shall inform her as soon as reasonably possible, close the current hearing, proceed as required by rules 61.2 and 63, and hear the original and the new *protests* together.

61.2 Protest Contents

A *protest* shall be in writing and identify

(a) the protestor and protestee;

(b) the incident, including where and when it occurred;

(c) any *rule* the protestor believes was broken; and

(d) the name of the protestor's representative.

However, if requirement (b) is met, requirement (a) may be met at any time before the hearing, and requirements (c) and (d) may be met before or during the hearing.

61.3 Protest Time Limit

A *protest* by a boat, or by the race committee or protest committee about an incident the committee observes in the racing area, shall be delivered to the race office no later than the time limit stated in the sailing instructions. If none is stated, the time limit is two hours after the last boat in the race *finishes*. Other race committee or protest committee *protests* shall be delivered to the race office within two hours after the committee receives the relevant information. The protest committee shall extend the time if there is good reason to do so.

62 REDRESS

62.1 A request for redress or a protest committee's decision to consider redress shall be based on a claim or possibility that a boat's score in a race or series has, through no fault of her own, been made significantly worse by

(a) an improper action or omission of the race committee, protest committee or organizing authority;

(b) injury or physical damage because of the action of a boat that was breaking a rule of Part 2 or of a vessel not *racing* that was required to keep clear;

(c) giving help (except to herself or her crew) in compliance with rule 1.1; or

(d) a boat against which a penalty has been imposed under rule 2 or disciplinary action has been taken under rule 69.1(b).

62.2 The request shall be made in writing within the time limit of rule 61.3 or within two hours of the relevant incident, whichever is later. The protest committee shall extend the time if there is good reason to do so. No red flag is required.

Section B - Hearings and Decisions

63 HEARINGS

63.1 Requirement for a Hearing

A boat or competitor shall not be penalized without a protest hearing, except as provided in rules 30.2, 30.3, 67, 69, A5 and P2. A decision on redress shall not be made without a hearing. The protest committee shall hear all *protests* and requests for redress that have been delivered to the race office unless it allows a *protest* or request to be withdrawn.

63.2 Time and Place of the Hearing; Time for Parties to Prepare

All *parties* to the hearing shall be notified of the time and place of the hearing, the *protest* or redress information shall be made available to them, and they shall be allowed reasonable time to prepare for the hearing.

63.3 Right to Be Present

(a) The *parties* to the hearing, or a representative of each, have the right to be present throughout the hearing of all the evidence. When a *protest* claims a breach of a rule of Part 2, 3 or 4, the representatives of boats shall have been on board at the time of the incident, unless there is good reason for the protest committee to rule otherwise. Any witness, other than a member of the protest committee, shall be excluded except when giving evidence.

(b) If a *party* to the hearing does not come to the hearing, the protest committee may nevertheless decide the *protest* or request for redress. If the *party* was unavoidably absent, the committee may reopen the hearing.

63.4 Interested Party

A member of a protest committee who is an *interested party* shall not take any further part in the hearing but may appear as a witness. A *party* to the hearing who believes a member of the protest committee is an *interested party* shall object as soon as possible.

63.5 Validity of the Protest or Request for Redress

At the beginning of the hearing the protest committee shall decide whether all requirements for the *protest* or request for redress have been met, after first taking any evidence it considers necessary. If all requirements have been met, the *protest* or request is valid and the hearing shall be continued. If not, it shall be closed. If the *protest* has been made under rule 60.3(a)(1), the protest committee shall also determine whether or not injury or serious damage resulted from the incident in question. If not, the hearing shall be closed.

63.6 Taking Evidence and Finding Facts

The protest committee shall take the evidence of the *parties* to the hearing and of their witnesses and other evidence it considers necessary. A member of the protest committee who saw the incident may give evidence. A *party* to the hearing may question any person who gives evidence. The committee shall then find the facts and base its decision on them.

63.7 Conflict between Rules

If there is a conflict between a *rule* in the notice of race and one in the sailing instructions that must be resolved before the protest committee can decide a *protest* or request for redress, the committee shall apply the *rule* that it believes will provide the fairest result for all boats affected.

63.8 Protests Between Boats in Different Races

A *protest* between boats sailing in different races conducted by different organizing authorities shall be heard by a protest committee acceptable to those authorities.

64 DECISIONS

64.1 Penalties and Exoneration

(a) When the protest committee decides that a boat that is a *party* to a protest hearing has broken a *rule*, it shall disqualify her unless some other penalty applies. A penalty shall be imposed whether or not the applicable rule was mentioned in the *protest*.

(b) When as a consequence of breaking a *rule* a boat has compelled another boat to break a *rule*, rule 64.1(a) does not apply to the other boat and she shall be exonerated.

(c) If a boat has broken a *rule* when not *racing*, her penalty shall apply to the race sailed nearest in time to that of the incident.

64.2 Decisions on Redress

When the protest committee decides that a boat is entitled to redress under rule 62, it shall make as fair an arrangement as possible for all boats affected, whether or not they asked for redress. This may be to adjust the scoring (see rule A10 for some examples) or finishing times of boats, to *abandon* the race, to let the results stand or to make some other arrangement. When in doubt about the facts or probable results of any arrangement for the race or series, especially before *abandoning* the race, the protest committee shall take evidence from appropriate sources.

64.3 Decisions on Measurement Protests

(a) When the protest committee finds that deviations in excess of tolerances specified in the class rules were caused by damage or normal wear and do not improve the performance of the boat, it shall not penalize her. However, the boat shall not *race* again until the deviations have been corrected, except when the protest committee decides there is or has been no reasonable opportunity to do so.

(b) When the protest committee is in doubt about the meaning of a measurement rule, it shall refer its questions, together with the relevant facts, to an authority responsible for interpreting the rule. In making its decision, the committee shall be bound by the reply of the authority.

(c) When a boat disqualified under a measurement rule states in writing that she intends to appeal, she may compete in subsequent races without changes to the boat, but shall be disqualified if she fails to appeal or the appeal is decided against her.

(d) Measurement costs arising from a *protest* involving a measurement rule shall be paid by the unsuccessful *party* unless the protest committee decides otherwise.

65 INFORMING THE PARTIES AND OTHERS

65.1 After making its decision, the protest committee shall promptly inform the *parties* to the hearing of the facts found, the applicable *rules*, the decision, the reasons for it, and any penalties imposed or redress given.

65.2 A *party* to the hearing is entitled to receive the above information in writing, provided she asks for it in writing from the protest committee within seven days of being informed of the decision. The committee shall then promptly provide the information, including, when relevant, a diagram of the incident prepared or endorsed by the committee.

65.3 When the protest committee penalizes a boat under a measurement rule, it shall send the above information to the relevant measurement authorities.

66 REOPENING A HEARING

The protest committee may reopen a hearing when it decides that it may have made a significant error, or when significant new evidence becomes available within a reasonable time. It shall reopen a hearing when required by the national authority under rule F5. A *party* to the hearing may ask for a reopening no later than 24 hours after being informed of the decision. When a hearing is reopened, a majority of the members of the protest committee shall, if possible, be members of the original protest committee.

67 RULE 42 AND HEARING REQUIREMENT

When so stated in the sailing instructions, the protest committee may penalize without a hearing a boat that has broken rule 42, provided that a member of the committee or its designated observer has seen the incident, and a disqualification under this rule shall not be excluded from the boat's series score. A boat so penalized shall be informed by notification in the race results.

RYA 68 DAMAGES

The question of damages arising from a breach of any *rule* shall be governed by the prescriptions, if any, of the national authority.

Section C - Gross Misconduct

69 ALLEGATIONS OF GROSS MISCONDUCT

69.1 Action by a Protest Committee

(a) When a protest committee, from its own observation or a report received from any source, believes that a competitor may have committed a gross breach of a *rule*, good manners or sportsmanship, or may have brought the sport into disrepute, it may call a hearing. The protest committee shall promptly inform the competitor in writing of the alleged misconduct and of the time and place of the hearing.

(b) A protest committee of at least three members shall conduct the hearing, following rules 63.2, 63.3, 63.4 and 63.6. If it decides that the competitor committed the alleged misconduct it shall either

(1) warn the competitor or

(2) impose a penalty by excluding the competitor and, when appropriate, disqualifying a boat, from a race or the remaining races or all races of the series, or by taking other action within its jurisdiction. A disqualification under this rule shall not be excluded from the boat's series score.

(c) The protest committee shall promptly report a penalty, but not a warning, to the national authorities of the venue, of the competitor and of the boat owner.

(d) If there is good reason for the competitor not to attend the hearing, the protest committee shall postpone it. However, if the competitor has left the event and as a result cannot reasonably be expected to attend a hearing, the protest committee shall not conduct one. Instead, it shall collect all available information and, if the allegation seems justified, make a report to the relevant national authorities.

(e) When the protest committee has left the event and a report alleging misconduct is received, the race committee or organizing authority may appoint a new protest committee to proceed under this rule.

69.2 Action by a National Authority

(a) When a national authority receives a report required by rule 69.1(c) or 69.1(d), a report alleging a gross breach of a *rule*, good manners or sportsmanship, or a report alleging conduct that has brought the sport into disrepute, it may conduct an investigation and, when appropriate, shall conduct a hearing. It may then take any disciplinary action within its jurisdiction it considers appropriate against the competitor or boat, or other person involved, including suspending eligibility, permanently or for a specified period of time, to compete in any event held within its jurisdiction, and suspending ISAF eligibility under ISAF Regulation 19.

(b) The national authority of a competitor shall also suspend the ISAF eligibility of the competitor as required in ISAF Regulation 19.

(c) The national authority shall promptly report a suspension of eligibility under rule 69.2(a) to the ISAF, and to the national authorities of the person or the owner of the boat suspended if they are not members of the suspending national authority.

69.3 Action by the ISAF

Upon receipt of a report required by rule 69.2(c) or ISAF Regulation 19, the ISAF shall inform all national authorities, which may also suspend eligibility for events held within their jurisdiction. The ISAF Executive Committee shall suspend the competitor's ISAF eligibility as required in ISAF Regulation 19 if the competitor's national authority does not do so.

Section D - Appeals

70 APPEALS; CONFIRMATION OR CORRECTION OF DECISIONS; RULE INTERPRETATIONS

70.1 Provided that the right of appeal has not been denied under rule 70.4, a *party* to a hearing may appeal a protest committee's decision or its procedures, but not the facts found, to the national authority of the venue.

70.2 A protest committee may request confirmation or correction of its decision.

70.3 A club or other organization affiliated to a national authority may request an interpretation of the *rules*, provided that no *protest* or request for redress that may be appealed is involved. The interpretation shall not be used for changing a previous protest committee decision.

RYA 70.4 There shall be no appeal from the decisions of an international jury constituted in compliance with Appendix N. Furthermore, if the notice of race and the sailing instructions so state, the right of appeal may be denied provided that

(a) it is essential to determine promptly the result of a race that will qualify a boat to compete in a later stage of an event or a subsequent event (a national authority may prescribe that its approval is required for such a procedure);

(b) a national authority so approves for a particular event open only to entrants under its own jurisdiction; or

(c) a national authority after consultation with the ISAF so approves for a particular event, provided the protest committee is constituted as required by Appendix N, except that only two members of the protest committee need be International Judges.

70.5 Appeals and requests shall conform to Appendix F.

71 APPEAL DECISIONS

71.1 No *interested party* or member of the protest committee shall take any part in the discussion or decision on an appeal or a request for confirmation or correction.

71.2 The national authority may uphold, change or reverse the protest committee's decision; declare the *protest* or request for redress invalid; or return the *protest* or request for the hearing to be reopened, or for a new hearing and decision by the same or a different protest committee.

71.3 When from the facts found by the protest committee the national authority decides that a boat that was a *party* to a protest hearing broke a *rule*, it shall penalize her, whether or not that boat or that *rule* was mentioned in the protest committee's decision.

71.4 The decision of the national authority shall be final. The national authority shall send its decision in writing to all *parties* to the hearing and the protest committee, who shall be bound by the decision.

PART 6
ENTRY AND QUALIFICATION

75 ENTERING A RACE

75.1 To enter a race, a boat shall comply with the requirements of the organizing authority of the race. She shall be entered by

(a) a member of a club or other organization affiliated to an ISAF member national authority,

(b) such a club or organization, or

(c) a member of an ISAF member national authority.

75.2 Competitors shall comply with ISAF Regulation 19, Eligibility Code.

76 EXCLUSION OF BOATS OR COMPETITORS

76.1 The organizing authority or the race committee may reject or cancel the entry of a boat or exclude a competitor, subject to rule 76.2, provided it does so before the start of the first race and states the reason for doing so. However, the organizing authority or the race committee shall not reject or cancel the entry of a boat or exclude a competitor because of advertising, provided the boat or competitor complies with ISAF Regulation 20, Advertising Code.

76.2 At world and continental championships no entry within stated quotas shall be rejected or cancelled without first obtaining the approval of the relevant international class association (or the Offshore Racing Council) or the ISAF.

77 IDENTIFICATION ON SAILS

A boat shall comply with the requirements of Appendix G governing class insignia, national letters and numbers on sails.

RYA 78 COMPLIANCE WITH CLASS RULES; CERTIFICATES

78.1 A boat's owner and any other person in charge shall ensure that the boat is maintained to comply with her class rules and that her measurement or rating certificate, if any, remains valid.

78.2 When a *rule* requires a certificate to be produced before a boat *races*, and it is not produced, the boat may *race* provided that the race committee receives a statement signed by the person in charge that a valid certificate exists and that it will be given to the race committee before the end of the event. If the certificate is not received in time, the boat shall be disqualified from all races of the event.

78.3 When a measurer for an event decides that a boat or personal equipment does not comply with the class rules, he shall report the matter in writing to the race committee, which shall protest the boat.

79 ADVERTISING

A boat and her crew shall comply with ISAF Regulation 20, Advertising Code.

80 RESCHEDULED RACES

When a race has been rescheduled, rule 36 applies and all boats entered in the original race shall be notified and, unless disqualified under rule 30.3, be entitled to sail the rescheduled race. New entries that meet the entry requirements of the original race may be accepted at the discretion of the race committee.

PART 7 - RACE ORGANIZATION

85 GOVERNING RULES

The organizing authority, race committee and protest committee shall be governed by the *rules* in the conduct and judging of races.

86 RULE CHANGES

86.1 A racing rule shall not be changed unless permitted in the rule itself or as follows:

(a) Prescriptions of a national authority may change a racing rule, but not the Definitions; a rule in the Introduction; Sportsmanship and the Rules; Part 1, 2 or 7; rule 42, 43.1, 43.2, 69, 70, 71, 75, 76.2 or 79; a rule of an appendix that changes one of these rules; Appendix H or N; or ISAF Regulation 19, 20 or 21.

(b) Sailing instructions may change a racing rule by referring specifically to it and stating the change, but not rule 76.1, Appendix F, or a rule listed in rule 86.1(a).

(c) Class rules may change only racing rules 42, 49, 50, 51, 52, 53 and 54.

86.2 In exception to rule 86.1, the ISAF may in limited circumstances (see ISAF Regulation 31.1.3) authorize changes to the racing rules for a specific international event. The authorization shall be stated in a letter of approval to the event organizing authority and in the notice of race and sailing instructions, and the letter shall be posted on the event's official notice board.

RYA 86.3 If a national authority so prescribes, these restrictions do not apply if rules are changed to develop or test proposed rules. The national authority may prescribe that its approval is required for such changes.

RYA 87 CHANGES TO NATIONAL AUTHORITY PRESCRIPTIONS

A national authority may restrict changes to its prescriptions with a prescription to this rule. If it does so, that prescription shall not be changed or deleted by sailing instructions.

88 ORGANIZING AUTHORITY; NOTICE OF RACE; APPOINTMENT OF RACE OFFICIALS

88.1 Organizing Authority

Races shall be organized by an organizing authority, which shall be

(a) the ISAF;

(b) a member national authority of the ISAF;

(c) a club or other organization affiliated to a national authority;

(d) a class association, either with the approval of a national authority or in conjunction with an affiliated club;

(e) an unaffiliated body in conjunction with an affiliated club where the body is owned and controlled by the club. The national authority of the club may prescribe that its approval is required for such an event; or

(f) if approved by the ISAF and the national authority of the club, an unaffiliated body in conjunction with an affiliated club where the body is not owned and controlled by the club.

88.2 Notice of Race; Appointment of Race Officials

(a) The organizing authority shall publish a notice of race that conforms to rule J1. The notice of race may be changed provided adequate notice is given.

(b) The organizing authority shall appoint a race committee and, when appropriate, appoint a protest committee and umpires. However, the race committee, an international jury and umpires may be appointed by the ISAF as provided in the ISAF regulations.

89 RACE COMMITTEE; SAILING INSTRUCTIONS; SCORING

89.1 Race Committee

The race committee shall conduct races as directed by the organizing authority and as required by the *rules*.

89.2 Sailing Instructions

(a) The race committee shall publish written sailing instructions that conform to rule J2.

(b) The sailing instructions for an international event shall include, in English, the applicable prescriptions of the national authority.

(c) Changes to the sailing instructions shall be in writing and posted within the required time on the official notice board or, on the water, communicated to each boat before her warning signal. Oral changes may be given only on the water, and only if the procedure is stated in the sailing instructions.

89.3 Scoring

(a) The race committee shall score a race or series as provided in Appendix A using the Low Point System, unless the sailing instructions specify the Bonus Point System or some other system. A race shall be scored if it is not *abandoned* and if one boat sails the course in compliance with rule 28.1 and *finishes* within the time limit, if any, even if she retires after *finishing* or is disqualified.

(b) When a scoring system provides for excluding one or more race scores from a boat's series score, the score for disqualification under rule 2; rule 30.3's next-to-last sentence; rule 42 if rule 67, P2.2 or P2.3 applies; or rule 69.1(b)(2) shall not be excluded. The next-worse score shall be excluded instead.

90 PROTEST COMMITTEE

A protest committee shall be

(a) a committee appointed by the organizing authority or race committee, or

(b) an international jury appointed by the organizing authority or as prescribed in the ISAF regulations and meeting the requirements of Appendix N. A national authority may prescribe that its approval is required for the appointment of international juries for races within its jurisdiction, except ISAF events or when international juries are appointed by the ISAF under rule 88.2(b).

APPENDIX A - SCORING

See rule 89.3.

A1 NUMBER OF RACES

The number of races scheduled and the number required to be completed to constitute a series shall be stated in the sailing instructions.

A2 SERIES SCORES

Each boat's series score shall be the total of her race scores excluding her worst score. (The sailing instructions may make a different arrangement by providing, for example, that no score will be excluded, that two or more scores will be excluded, or that a specified number of scores will be excluded if a specified number of races are completed. A race is completed if scored; see rule 89.3(a).) If a boat has two or more equal worst scores, the score(s) for the race(s) sailed earliest in the series shall be excluded. The boat with the lowest series score wins and others shall be ranked accordingly.

A3 STARTING TIMES AND FINISHING PLACES

The time of a boat's starting signal shall be her starting time, and the order in which boats *finish* a race shall determine their finishing places. However, when a handicap or rating system is used a boat's corrected time shall determine her finishing place.

A4 LOW POINT AND BONUS POINT SYSTEMS

Most series are scored using either the Low Point System or the Bonus Point System. The Low Point System uses a boat's finishing place as her race score. The Bonus Point System benefits the first six finishers because of the greater difficulty in advancing from fourth place to third, for example, than from fourteenth place to thirteenth. The Low Point System will apply unless the sailing instructions specify another system; see rule 89.3(a). If the Bonus Point System is chosen it can be made to apply by stating in the sailing instructions that 'The Bonus Point System of Appendix A will apply.'

A4.1 Each boat *starting* and *finishing* and not thereafter retiring, being penalized or given redress shall be scored points as follows:

Finishing place	*Low Point System*	*Bonus Point System*
First	1	0
Second	2	3
Third	3	5.7
Fourth	4	8
Fifth	5	10
Sixth	6	11.7
Seventh	7	13
Each place thereafter	Add 1 point	Add 1 point

A4.2 A boat that did not *start*, did not *finish*, retired after *finishing* or was disqualified shall be scored points for the finishing place one more than the number of boats entered in the series. A boat penalized under rule 30.2 or 44.3 shall be scored points as provided in rule 44.3(c).

A5 SCORES DETERMINED BY THE RACE COMMITTEE

A boat that did not *start*, comply with rule 30.2 or 30.3, or *finish*, or that takes a penalty under rule 44.3 or retires after *finishing*, shall be scored accordingly by the race committee without a hearing. Only the protest committee may take other scoring actions that worsen a boat's score.

A6 CHANGES IN PLACES AND SCORES OF OTHER BOATS

A6.1 If a boat is disqualified from a race or retires after *finishing*, each boat with a worse finishing place shall be moved up one place.

A6.2 If the protest committee decides to give redress by adjusting a boat's score, the scores of other boats shall not be changed unless the protest committee decides otherwise.

A7 RACE TIES

If boats are tied at the finishing line or if a handicap or rating system is used and boats have equal corrected times, the points for the place for which the boats have tied and for the place(s) immediately below shall be added together and divided equally. Boats tied for a race prize shall share it or be given equal prizes.

A8 SERIES TIES

A8.1 If there is a series score tie between two or more boats, each boat's race scores shall be listed in order of best to worst, and at the first point(s) where there is a difference the tie shall be broken in favour of the boat(s) with the best score(s). No excluded scores shall be used.

A8.2 If a tie remains between two or more boats, they shall be ranked in order of their scores in the last race. Any remaining ties shall be broken by using the tied boats' scores in the next-to-last race and so on until all ties are broken. These scores shall be used even if some of them are excluded scores.

A9 RACE SCORES IN A SERIES LONGER THAN A REGATTA

For a series that is held over a period of time longer than a regatta, a boat that came to the starting area but did not *start*, did not *finish*, retired after *finishing* or was disqualified shall be scored points for the finishing place one more than the number of boats that came to the starting area. A boat that did not come to the starting area shall be scored points for the finishing place one more than the number of boats entered in the series.

A10 GUIDANCE ON REDRESS

If the protest committee decides to give redress by adjusting a boat's score for a race, it is advised to consider scoring her

(a) points equal to the average, to the nearest tenth of a point (0.05 to be rounded upward), of her points in all the races in the series except the race in question;

(b) points equal to the average, to the nearest tenth of a point (0.05 to be rounded upward), of her points in all the races before the race in question; or

(c) points based on the position of the boat in the race at the time of the incident that justified redress.

A11 SCORING ABBREVIATIONS

These abbreviations are recommended for recording the circumstances described:

DNC	Did not *start*; did not come to the starting area
DNS	Did not *start* (other than DNC and OCS)
OCS	Did not *start*; on the course side of the starting line at her starting signal and failed to *start*, or broke rule 30.1
ZFP	20% penalty under rule 30.2
BFD	Disqualification under rule 30.3
SCP	Took a scoring penalty under rule 44.3
DNF	Did not *finish*
RAF	Retired after *finishing*
DSQ	Disqualification
DNE	Disqualification (other than DGM) not excludable under rule 89.3(b)
DGM	Disqualification under rule 69.1(b)(2); not excludable
RDG	Redress given

APPENDIX B
WINDSURFING COMPETITION RULES

Windsurfing competition shall be sailed under The Racing Rules of Sailing *as changed by this appendix. The term 'boat' elsewhere in the racing rules means 'board' or 'boat' as appropriate. A windsurfing event can include one or more of the following disciplines or their formats:*

Discipline	Formats
Racing	*Course racing; slalom; marathon*
Expression	*Wave performance; freestyle*
Speed	

In expression competition a board's performance is judged on skill and variety rather than speed and is organized using elimination series. Either wave performance or freestyle competition is organized, depending on the wave conditions at the venue. In speed competition, a 'round' consists of one or more speed runs in which the boards take turns sailing the course at intervals. In the racing discipline a marathon race is a race scheduled to last more than one hour.

In slalom racing or expression competition, 'heat' means one elimination contest, a 'round' consists of one or more heats, and an elimination series consists of a maximum of four rounds.

B1 DEFINITIONS

B1.1 The following additional definitions apply:

Beach Start When the starting line is on the beach, or so close to the beach that the competitor must stand in the water to *start*, the start is a *beach start*.

Capsized A board is *capsized* when her sail or the competitor is in the water.

B1.2 The following definitions apply only to expression competition:

Coming In and Going Out A board sailing in the same direction as the incoming surf is *coming in*. A board sailing in the direction opposite to the incoming surf is *going out*.

Jumping A board is *jumping* when she takes off at the top of a wave while *going out*.

Overtaking A board is *overtaking* from the moment she gains an *overlap* from *clear astern* until the moment she is *clear ahead* of the *overtaken* board.

Possession The first board sailing shoreward immediately in front of a wave has *possession* of that wave. However, when it is impossible to determine which board is first the *windward* board has *possession*.

Recovering A board is *recovering* from the time her sail or, when water-starting, the competitor is out of the water until she has steerage way.

Surfing A board is *surfing* when she is on or immediately in front of a wave while *coming in*.

Transition A board changing *tacks*, or taking off while *coming in*, or one that is not *surfing, jumping, capsized* or *recovering* is in *transition*.

B2 RULES FOR ALL COMPETITION

B2.1 Changes to the Rules of Part 4

(a) Rule 42 is changed to 'A board shall be propelled only by the action of the wind on the sail, by the action of the water on the hull and by the unassisted actions of the competitor.'

(b) Add to rule 43.1(a): 'However, a competitor may wear a drinking container that shall have a capacity of at least one litre and weigh no more than 1.5 kilograms when full.'

(c) Rule 44.2 is changed so that two turns are replaced by one 360° turn with no requirement for tacks or gybes.

(d) Rules 44.3 and 44.4(a) are deleted.

(e) Add to rule 47.1: 'except as stated in rule 41.2'. (See rule B4.4.) Rule 47.2 is deleted.

B2.2 Entry and Qualification

Add to rule 78.1: 'When so prescribed by the ISAF, a numbered and dated device on a board and her centreboard, fin and rig shall serve as her measurement certificate.'

B2.3 Event Organization

(a) The last sentence of rule 89.2(c) is deleted.

(b) Add new rule 89.2(d): 'Oral instructions may be given only if the procedure is stated in the sailing instructions.'

B2.4 Identification on Sails

(a) Add to rule G1.1(a): 'The insignia shall not refer to anything other than the manufacturer or class and shall not consist of more than two letters and three numbers or an abstract design.'

(b) Rules G1.3(a), G1.3(c), G1.3(d) and G1.3(e) are changed to

The class insignia shall be displayed once on each side of the sail in the area above a line projected at right angles from a point on the luff of the sail one-third of the distance from the head to the wishbone. The national letters and sail numbers shall be in the central third of that part of the sail above the wishbone, clearly separated from any advertising, and placed at different heights on the two sides of the sail, those on the starboard side being uppermost.

B3 RULES FOR RACING COMPETITION

B3.1 When Boards Meet

(a) Rule 13 becomes rule 13.1. Add new rule 13.2:

A board gybing shall *keep clear* of other boards. During that time rules 10, 11 and 12 do not apply. If two boards are subject to this rule at the same time, the one on the other's port side or the one astern shall *keep clear*.

(b) Rules 17, 18.2(b), 18.2(c) and 18.3 are deleted.

(c) Rule 21 becomes rule 21.1. Add new rule 21.2: 'A *capsized* board shall not take an action that hinders another board.'

(d) Add new rule 22.3: 'A board shall not sail in the course area defined in the sailing instructions when races are taking place except in her own race.'

(e) Add new rule 23:

23 SAIL OUT OF THE WATER WHEN STARTING

When approaching the starting line to *start*, a board shall have her sail out of the water and in a normal position, except when accidentally *capsized.*

B3.2 Starting Races

The sailing instructions shall specify one of these starting systems.

(a) SYSTEM 1

See rule 26, Starting Races.

(b) SYSTEM 2

Races shall be started by using the following signals. Times shall be taken from the visual signals; the absence of a sound signal shall be disregarded.

Signal	*Flag*	*Sound*	*Minutes before starting signal*
Attention	Class flag or heat number		5
	Attention signal removed		4
Warning	Red flag	1 sound	3
	Red flag removed		2
Preparatory	Yellow flag	1 sound	1
	Yellow flag removed		1/2
Starting	Green flag	1 sound	0

(c) SYSTEM 3 (FOR BEACH STARTS)

(1) Before her start each board in a heat or class shall draw a number for her station on the starting line. The stations shall be numbered so that station 1 is the most windward one.

(2) After boards have been called to take their positions, the race committee shall make the preparatory signal by displaying a red flag with one sound. The starting signal shall be made, at any time after the preparatory signal, by removing the red flag with one sound.

(3) After the starting signal each board shall take the shortest route from her starting station to her windsurfing position in the water (with both of the competitor's feet on the board).

B3.3 Other Rules for the Conduct of a Race

(a) Add new rule 29.3:

29.3 Recall for a Slalom Race

(a) When at a board's starting signal for a slalom race or heat any part of her hull, crew or equipment is on the course side of the starting line, the race committee shall signal a general recall.

(b) If the race committee acts under rule 29.3(a) and the board is identified, she shall be disqualified without a hearing, even if the race or heat is *postponed* or *abandoned*. The race committee shall hail or display her sail number, and she shall leave the course area immediately. If the race or heat is restarted or resailed, she shall not sail in it.

(b) Change rule 31 to 'A board may touch a *mark* but shall not hold on to it.'

B4 RULES FOR EXPRESSION COMPETITION

B4.1 Right-of-Way Rules

These rules replace all rules of Part 2.

(a) COMING IN AND GOING OUT

A board *coming in* shall *keep clear* of a board *going out*. When two boards are *going out* or *coming in* while on the same wave, or when neither is *going out* or *coming in*, the board on *port tack* shall *keep clear* of the one on *starboard tack*.

(b) BOARDS ON THE SAME WAVE, COMING IN

When two or more boards are on a wave *coming in*, a board that does not have *possession* shall *keep clear*.

(c) CLEAR ASTERN, CLEAR AHEAD AND OVERTAKING

A board *clear astern* and not on a wave shall *keep clear* of a board *clear ahead*. An *overtaking* board that is not on a wave shall *keep clear*.

(d) TRANSITION

A board in *transition* shall *keep clear* of one that is not. When two boards are in *transition* at the same time, the one on the other's port side or the one astern shall *keep clear*.

B4.2 Starting and Ending Heats

Heats shall be started and ended by using the following signals:

(a) STARTING A HEAT

Each flag shall be removed when the next flag is displayed.

Signal	*Flag*	*Sound*	*Minutes before starting signal*
Attention	Heat number		3
Warning	Red flag	1 sound	2
Preparatory	Yellow flag	1 sound	1
Starting	Green flag	1 sound	0

(b) ENDING A HEAT

Signal	*Flag*	*Sound*	*Minutes before ending signal*
End warning	Green flag removed	1 sound	1
Ending	Red flag	1 sound	0

B4.3 Registration of Sails; Course Area; Heat Duration

(a) Boards shall register with the race committee the colours and other particulars of their sails, or their identification according to another method stated in the sailing instructions, no later than the starting signal for the heat two heats before their own.

(b) The course area shall be defined in the sailing instructions and posted on the official notice board not later than 30 minutes before the starting signal for the first heat. A board shall be scored only while sailing in the course area.

(c) Any change in heat duration shall be announced by the race committee not later than fifteen minutes before the starting signal for the first heat in the next round.

B4.4 Outside Help

Rule 41 becomes rule 41.1. Add new rule 41.2:

> An assistant may provide replacement equipment to a board but shall keep clear of other boards competing. A board whose assistant fails to keep clear shall be penalized. The penalty shall be at the discretion of the protest committee.

B5 ELIMINATION SERIES FOR SLALOM RACING AND EXPRESSION COMPETITION

Rules B5.1 – B5.5 apply to slalom racing or expression competition organized by using elimination series in which boards compete in heats.

B5.1 Elimination Series Procedure

(a) Competition shall take the form of one or more elimination series. Each of them shall consist of either a maximum of four rounds in a single elimination series where only a number of the best scorers advance, or a maximum of ten rounds in a double elimination series where boards have more than one opportunity to advance.

(b) Boards shall sail one against another in pairs, or in groups determined by the elimination ladder. The selected form of competition shall not be changed while a round remains uncompleted.

B5.2 Seeding and Ranking Lists

(a) When a seeding or ranking list is used to establish the heats of the first round, places 1–8 (four heats) or 1–16 (eight heats) shall be distributed evenly among the heats.

(b) For a subsequent elimination series, if any, boards shall be reassigned to new heats according to a seeding list based on the current overall standings.

(c) The organizing authority's seeding decisions are final and are not grounds for a request for redress.

B5.3 Heat Schedule

The schedule of heats shall be posted on the official notice board not later than 30 minutes before the starting signal for the first heat.

B5.4 Advancement and Byes

(a) In slalom racing and freestyle competition, the boards in each heat to advance to the next round shall be announced by the race committee not later than 30 minutes before the starting signal for the first heat. The number advancing may be changed by the protest committee as a result of a redress decision.

(b) In expression competition, any first-round byes shall be assigned to the highest-seeded boards.

(c) In wave performance competition, only the winner of each heat shall advance to the next round.

(d) In freestyle competition, boards shall advance to the next round as follows: from an eight-board heat, the best four advance, and the winner will sail against the fourth and the second against the third; from a four-board heat, the best two advance and will sail against each other.

B5.5 Finals

(a) The final shall consist of a maximum of three races. The race committee shall announce the number of races to be sailed in the final not later than five minutes before the warning signal for the first final race.

(b) A runners-up final may be sailed after the final. All boards in the semifinal heats that failed to qualify for the final may compete in it.

B6 RULES FOR SPEED COMPETITION

B6.1 General Rules

All rules of Part 2 are replaced by relevant parts of this rule.

(a) BEACH AND WATER STARTING

A board shall not *beach start* or water start on the course or in the starting area, except to sail off the course to avoid boards that are *starting* or *racing*.

(b) LEAVING THE COURSE AREA

A board leaving the course area shall *keep clear* of boards *racing*.

(c) COURSE CONTROL

When the race committee points an orange flag at a board, she shall immediately leave the course area.

(d) RETURNING TO THE STARTING AREA

A board returning to the starting area shall keep clear of the course.

(e) RUN; ROUND

The maximum number of runs to be made by each board in

a round shall be announced by the race committee not later than 30 minutes before the starting signal for the first round.

(f) DURATION OF A ROUND

The duration of a round shall be announced by the race committee not later than 30 minutes before the starting signal for the next round.

(g) CONDITIONS FOR ESTABLISHING A RECORD

The minimum distance for a world record is 500 metres. Other records may be established over shorter distances. The course shall be defined by posts and transits ashore or by buoys afloat. Transits shall not converge.

B6.2 Starting System for Speed Competition

Rounds shall be started and ended by using the following signals. Each flag shall be removed when the next flag is displayed.

(a) STARTING A ROUND

Signal	*Flag*	*Meaning*
Stand-by	Red flag	Course closed
Course closed	AP and red flag	Course closed; will open shortly
Preparatory	Yellow flag	Course will open in 5 minutes
Starting	Green flag	Course is open

(b) ENDING A ROUND

Signal	*Flag*	*Meaning*
End warning	Green and yellow flag	Course will be closed in 5 minutes
Extension	Green flag and L	Current round extended by 15 minutes
Round ended	Red flag and L	A new round will be started shortly

B6.3 Penalties

(a) If a board fails to comply with a warning by the race committee, she may be cautioned and her sail number shall be posted on a notice board near the finishing line.

(b) If a board is cautioned a second time during the same round, she shall be suspended by the race committee from the remainder of the round and her sail number shall be posted on the official notice board.

(c) A board observed in the course area while suspended shall be disqualified from the competition without a hearing and none of her previous times or results shall be valid.

(d) Any breach of the verification rules may result in a suspension from the competition for any period.

B6.4 Verification

(a) An observer appointed by the World Sailing Speed Record Council (WSSRC) shall be present and verify run times and speeds at world record attempts. The race committee shall verify run times and speeds at other record attempts.

(b) A competitor shall not enter the timing control area or discuss any timing matter directly with the timing organization. Any timing question shall be directed to the race committee.

B7 PROTESTS, REDRESS, HEARINGS AND APPEALS

B7.1 (a) Add after the third sentence of rule 61.1(a): 'She shall inform the race committee of her intention to protest immediately after she *finishes* or retires.'

(b) Rule 61.2 is retitled rule 61.2(a), Course and Marathon Racing.

Add new rule 61.2(b):

SLALOM RACING AND OTHER DISCIPLINES

A *protest* shall be made orally immediately following the heat in which the incident occurred.

B7.2 Add new rule 62.1(e): 'a board that failed to *keep clear* and retired or was penalized.'

B7.3 In rule 62.2, after 'writing' add: 'except in an elimination series'.

B7.4 Rule 63.2 becomes rule 63.2(a). Add new rule 63.2(b): 'In an elimination series, the protest committee may hear a *protest* on the beach or water immediately after the heat.'

B7.5 Begin rule 65.2 with the addition 'Except in an elimination series'.

B7.6 Rule 67 is deleted.

B7.7 Add new rule 70.6: 'Appeals are not permitted in slalom racing and expression competition.'

B8 SCORING

B8.1 Overall Scores

If an event includes more than one discipline or format the sailing instructions shall state how the overall score is to be calculated.

B8.2 Series Scores

Rule A2 is changed to

Each board's series score shall be the total of her race, elimination series or speed round scores with the number of her worst scores excluded as follows:

Course races, speed rounds	*Slalom and expression elimination series*	*Number excluded*
1–3	1–2	0
4–6	3–4	1
7–10	5–7	2
11–15	8 or more	3
16 or more		4

If a board has two or more equal worst scores, the score(s) for the race(s) sailed earliest in the series shall be excluded. The board with the lowest series score wins and others shall be ranked accordingly. Rules B8.5, B8.6 and B8.7 contain exceptions to this rule.

B8.3 Scoring Systems

(a) Rule A4 is retitled 'Low Point and Alternative Systems' and its preamble is deleted. Rule A4.1 is changed to

Each board *starting* and *finishing* and not thereafter retiring, being penalized or given redress shall be scored points as follows:

Finishing place	*Low Point System*	*Alternative System*
First	1	0.7
Second	2	2
Third	3	3
Each place thereafter	Add 1 point	Add 1 point

(b) Add to the end of the first sentence of rule A4.2: 'or, in an elimination series, the number of boards in that heat'.

B8.4 Uncompleted Heat

When a heat cannot be completed, the points for the unscored places shall be added together and divided by the number of places in that heat. The resulting number of points, to the nearest tenth of a point (0.05 to be rounded upward), shall be given to each board entered in the heat.

B8.5 Scoring a Final Series in Slalom

(a) If three final races are completed, a board's series score in the final shall be the total of her race scores excluding her worst score. Otherwise her series score shall be the total of her race scores.

(b) A board that did not *start*, did not *finish*, retired after *finishing* or was disqualified from a final race shall be scored points equal to the total number of boards entered in the final.

B8.6 Expression Competition Scoring

(a) Expression competition shall be scored by a panel of three judges. However, the panel may have a greater odd number of members, and there may be two such panels. Each judge shall give points for each manoeuvre based on the scale stated in the sailing instructions.

(b) The criteria of scoring shall be decided by the race committee and announced on the official notice board not later than 30 minutes before the starting signal for the first heat.

(c) A board's heat standing shall be determined by adding together the points given by each judge. The board with the highest score wins and others shall be ranked accordingly.

(d) Both semifinal heats shall have been sailed for an elimination series to be valid.

(e) Except for members of the race committee responsible for scoring the event, only competitors in the heat shall be allowed to see judges' score sheets for the heat. Each score sheet shall bear the full name of the judge.

(f) Scoring decisions of the judges shall not be grounds for a request for redress by a board.

B8.7 Speed Competition

The speeds of a board's fastest two runs in a round shall be averaged to determine her standing in that round. The board with the highest average wins and others shall be ranked accordingly.

B8.8 Series Ties

(a) RACING AND SPEED COMPETITION

Rule A8 is changed as follows for racing and speed competition:

(1) Add new rule A8.1: 'If there is a series score tie between two or more boards, it shall be broken in favour of the board(s) with the best single excluded race score(s).'

(2) Rule A8.1 becomes rule A8.2. Its beginning 'If there is a series score tie' is changed to 'If a tie remains' and its last sentence is changed to 'These scores shall be used even if some of them are excluded scores.'

(3) Rule A8.2 becomes rule A8.3 and its beginning ‘If a tie remains’ is changed to ‘If a tie still remains’.

(b) EXPRESSION COMPETITION

Rule A8 is changed as follows for expression competition:

(1) In a heat, if there is a tie in the total points given by one or more judges, it shall be broken in favour of the board with the higher single score in the priority category. If the categories are weighted equally, in wave performance competition the tie shall be broken in favour of the board with the higher single score in wave riding, and in freestyle competition in favour of the board with the higher score for overall impression. If a tie remains, in wave performance competition it shall be broken in favour of the board with the higher single score in the category without priority, and in freestyle competition it shall stand as the final result.

(2) If there is a tie in the series score, it shall be broken in favour of the board that scored better more times than the other board. All scores shall be used even if some of them are excluded scores.

(3) If a tie still remains, the heat shall be resailed. If this is not possible, the tie shall stand as the final result.

APPENDIX C
MATCH RACING RULES

Match races shall be sailed under The Racing Rules of Sailing *as changed by this appendix. Matches shall be umpired unless the notice of race and sailing instructions state otherwise.*

C1 TERMINOLOGY

'Competitor' means the skipper, team or boat as appropriate for the event. 'Flight' means two or more matches started in the same starting sequence.

C2 CHANGES TO THE DEFINITIONS AND THE RULES OF PARTS 2 AND 4

C2.1 The definition *Finish* is changed to:

> A boat *finishes* when any part of her hull, or crew or equipment in normal position, crosses the finishing line in the direction of the course from the last *mark* after completing any penalties. However, when penalties are cancelled under rule C7.2(d) after one or both boats have *finished* each shall be recorded as *finished* when she crossed the line.

C2.2 Add to the definition *Proper Course:* 'A boat taking a penalty or manoeuvring to take a penalty is not sailing a *proper course*.'

C2.3 The last sentence of the definition *Clear Ahead* and *Clear Astern*; *Overlap* is changed to 'These terms do not apply to boats on opposite *tacks* unless either rule 18 applies or both boats are subject to rule 13.2.'

C2.4 Rule 13 is changed to

13 WHILE TACKING OR GYBING

13.1 After a boat passes head to wind, she shall *keep clear* of other boats until she is on a close-hauled course.

13.2 After the foot of the mainsail of a boat sailing downwind crosses the centreline she shall *keep clear* of other boats until her mainsail has filled.

13.3 While rule 13.1 or 13.2 applies, rules 10, 11 and 12 do not. However, if two boats are subject to rule 13.1 or 13.2 at the same time, the one on the other's port side or the one astern shall *keep clear*.

C2.5 Rules 16.2 and 17.2 are deleted.

C2.6 Rule 18.3 is changed to

If two boats were on opposite *tacks* and one of them completes a tack within the *two-length zone* to pass a rounding *mark*, and if thereafter the other boat cannot by luffing avoid becoming *overlapped* inside her, the boat that tacked shall *keep clear* and rules 15 and 18.2 do not apply. If the other boat can by luffing avoid becoming *overlapped* inside her then rule 18.2(c) shall apply as if the boats were *clear ahead* and *clear astern* at the *two-length zone*.

C2.7 When rule 19.1 applies, the following arm signals by the helmsman are required in addition to the hails:

(a) for 'Room to tack', repeatedly and clearly pointing to windward; and

(b) for 'You tack', repeatedly and clearly pointing at the other boat and waving the arm to windward.

C2.8 Rule 20.2 is changed to 'A boat taking a penalty shall *keep clear* of one that is not.'

C2.9 Rule 22.1 is changed to 'If reasonably possible, a boat not *racing* shall not interfere with a boat that is *racing* or an umpire boat.'

C2.10 Rule 22.2 is changed to 'Except when sailing a *proper course*, a boat shall not interfere with a boat taking a penalty or sailing on another leg.'

C2.11 Add new rule 22.3: 'When boats in different matches meet, any change of course by either boat shall be consistent with complying with a *rule* or trying to win her own match.'

C2.12 Add to the preamble of Part 4: 'Rule 42 shall also apply between the warning and preparatory signals.'

C2.13 Rule 42.2(d) is changed to 'sculling: repeated movement of the helm to propel the boat forward;'.

C3 RACE SIGNALS AND CHANGES TO RELATED RULES

C3.1 Starting Signals

The signals for starting a match shall be as follows. Times shall be taken from the visual signals; the failure of a sound signal shall be disregarded. If more than one match will be sailed, the starting signal for one match shall be the warning signal for the next match.

Time in minutes	*Visual signal*	*Sound signal*	*Means*
10	Flag F displayed	One	Attention signal
6	Flag F removed	None	
5	Numeral pennant displayed*	One	Warning signal
4	Flag P displayed	One	Preparatory signal
2	Blue or yellow flag or both displayed**	One**	End of pre-start entry time
0	Warning and preparatory signals removed	One	Starting signal

* Within a flight, numeral pennant 1 means Match 1, pennant 2 means Match 2, etc., unless the sailing instructions state otherwise.

** These signals shall be made only if one or both boats fail to comply with rule C4.2. The flag(s) shall be displayed until the umpires have signalled a penalty or for one minute, whichever is earlier.

C3.2 **Changes to Related Rules**

(a) Rule 29.1 is changed to

(1) When at a boat's starting signal any part of her hull, crew or equipment is on the course side of the starting line or its extensions, the race committee shall promptly display a blue or yellow flag identifying the boat with one sound. The flag shall be displayed until the boat is completely on the pre-start side of the starting line or its extensions or until two minutes after her starting signal, whichever is earlier.

(2) When at a boat's starting signal no part of her hull, crew or equipment is on the course side of the starting line or its extensions, and before she *starts* she sails to the course side across an extension, the race committee shall promptly display a blue or yellow flag identifying the boat. The flag shall be displayed until the boat is completely on the pre-start side of the starting line or its extensions or until two minutes after her starting signal, whichever is earlier.

(b) In the race signal AP the last sentence is changed to 'The attention signal will be made 1 minute after removal unless at that time the race is *postponed* again or *abandoned*.'

(c) In the race signal N the last sentence is changed to 'The attention signal will be made 1 minute after removal unless at that time the race is *postponed* again or *abandoned*.'

C3.3 **Finishing Line Signals**

The race signal Blue flag or shape shall not be used.

C4 REQUIREMENTS BEFORE THE START

C4.1 At her preparatory signal, each boat shall be outside the line that is at a 90° angle to the starting line through the starting *mark* at her assigned end. In the race schedule pairing list, the boat listed on the left-hand side is assigned the port end and shall display a blue flag at her stern while *racing*. The other boat is assigned the starboard end and shall display a yellow flag at her stern while *racing*.

C4.2 Within the two-minute period following her preparatory signal, a boat shall cross and clear the starting line, the first time from the course side to the pre-start side.

C5 SIGNALS BY UMPIRES

C5.1 A green and white flag with one long sound means 'No penalty.'

C5.2 A blue or yellow flag identifying a boat with one long sound means 'The identified boat shall take a penalty by complying with rule C7.'

C5.3 A red flag with or soon after a blue or yellow flag with one long sound means 'The identified boat shall take a penalty by complying with rule C7.3(d).'

C5.4 A black flag with a blue or yellow flag and one long sound means 'The identified boat is disqualified, and the match is terminated and awarded to the other boat.'

C5.5 One short sound means 'A penalty is now completed.'

C5.6 Repetitive short sounds mean 'A boat is no longer taking a penalty and the penalty remains.'

C5.7 A blue or yellow flag or shape displayed from an umpire boat means 'The identified boat has an outstanding penalty.'

C6 PROTESTS AND REQUESTS FOR REDRESS BY BOATS

C6.1 A boat may protest another boat

(a) under a rule of Part 2, except rule 14, by clearly displaying flag Y immediately after an incident in which she was involved;

(b) under any rule not listed in rule C6.1(a) or C6.2 by clearly displaying a red flag as soon as possible after the incident.

C6.2 A boat may not protest another boat under

(a) rule 14, unless damage results;

(b) a rule of Part 2, unless she was involved in the incident;

(c) rule 31 or 42; or

(d) rule C4 or C7.

C6.3 A boat intending to request redress because of circumstances that arise before she *finishes* or retires shall clearly display a red flag as soon as possible after she becomes aware of those circumstances, but not later than two minutes after *finishing* or retiring.

C6.4 (a) A boat protesting under rule C6.1(a) shall remove flag Y before or as soon as possible after the umpires' signal.

(b) A boat protesting under rule C6.1(b) or requesting redress under rule C6.3 shall, for her *protest* or request to be valid, keep her red flag displayed until she has so informed the umpires after *finishing* or retiring. No written *protest* or request for redress is required.

C6.5 **Umpire Decisions**

(a) After flag Y is displayed, the umpires shall decide whether to penalize any boat. They shall signal their decision in compliance with rule C5.1, C5.2 or C5.3.

(b) The red-flag penalty in rule C5.3 shall be used when a boat has gained control as a result of breaking a *rule*, but the umpires are not certain that the conditions for an additional umpire-initiated penalty have been fulfilled.

C6.6 **Protest Committee Decisions**

(a) The protest committee may take evidence in any way it considers appropriate and may communicate its decision orally.

(b) If the protest committee decides that a breach of a *rule* has had no significant effect on the outcome of the match, it may

(1) impose a penalty of one point or part of one point;

(2) order a resail; or

(3) make another arrangement it decides is equitable, which may be to impose no penalty.

(c) The penalty for breaking rule 14 when damage or injury results will be at the discretion of the protest committee, and may include exclusion from further races in the event.

C7 PENALTY SYSTEM

C7.1 Rule Changes

Rules 31.2 and 44 are deleted.

C7.2 All Penalties

(a) A penalized boat may delay taking a penalty within the limitations of rule C7.3 and shall take it as follows:

(1) When on a leg of the course to a windward *mark*, she shall gybe and, as soon as reasonably possible, luff to a close-hauled course.

(2) When on a leg of the course to a leeward *mark* or the finishing line, she shall tack and, as soon as reasonably possible, bear away to a downwind course.

(b) Add to rule 2: 'When *racing*, a boat may wait for an umpire's decision before taking a penalty.'

(c) A boat completes a leg of the course when her bow crosses the extension of the line from the previous *mark* through the *mark* she is rounding, or on the last leg when she *finishes*.

(d) A penalized boat shall not be recorded as having *finished* until she takes her penalty and sails completely to the course side of the line and then *finishes*, unless the penalty is cancelled before or after she crosses the finishing line.

(e) If a boat has one or two outstanding penalties and the other boat in her match is penalized, one penalty for each boat shall be cancelled except that a red-flag penalty shall not cancel an outstanding penalty.

(f) If a boat has more than two outstanding penalties, the umpires shall signal her disqualification under rule C5.4.

C7.3 Penalty Limitations

(a) A boat taking a penalty that includes a tack shall have the spinnaker head below the main-boom gooseneck from the time she passes head to wind until she is on a close-hauled course.

(b) No part of a penalty may be taken within two of a boat's hull lengths of a rounding *mark*.

(c) If a boat has one outstanding penalty, she may take the penalty any time after *starting* and before *finishing*. If a boat has two outstanding penalties, she shall take one of them as soon as reasonably possible, but not before *starting*.

(d) When the umpires display a red flag with or soon after a penalty flag, the penalized boat shall take a penalty as soon as reasonably possible, but not before *starting*.

C7.4 Taking and Completing Penalties

(a) When a boat with an outstanding penalty is on a leg to a windward *mark* and gybes, or is on a leg to a leeward *mark* or the finishing line and passes head to wind, she is taking a penalty.

(b) When a boat taking a penalty either does not take the penalty correctly or does not complete the penalty as soon as reasonably possible, she is no longer taking a penalty. The umpires shall signal this as required by rule C5.6.

(c) The umpire boat for each match shall display blue or yellow flags or shapes, each flag or shape indicating one outstanding penalty. When a boat has taken a penalty, or a penalty has been cancelled, one flag or shape shall be removed. Failure of the umpires to display or remove flags or shapes shall not change the number of penalties outstanding.

C8 PENALTIES INITIATED BY UMPIRES

C8.1 Rule Changes

(a) Rules 60.2(a) and 60.3(a) do not apply to *rules* for which penalties may be imposed by umpires.

(b) Rule 64.1(b) is changed so that the provision for exonerating a boat may be applied by the umpires without a hearing, and it takes precedence over any conflicting rule of this appendix.

C8.2 When the umpires decide that a boat has broken rule 31, 42, C4, C7.3(c) or C7.3(d) she shall be penalized by signalling her under rule C5.2 or C5.3. However, a boat that displays an incorrect flag or does not display the correct flag shall be warned orally and given an opportunity to correct the error before being penalized.

C8.3 When the umpires decide that a boat has

(a) gained an advantage by breaking a *rule* after allowing for a penalty,

(b) deliberately broken a *rule*, or

(c) committed a breach of sportsmanship,

she shall be penalized under rule C5.2, C5.3 or C5.4.

C8.4 If the umpires or protest committee members decide that a boat may have broken a *rule* other than those listed in rules C6.1(a) and C6.2, they shall so inform the protest committee for its action under rule 60.3 and rule C6.6 when appropriate.

C8.5 When, after one boat has started, the umpires are satisfied that the other boat will not *start*, they may signal under rule C5.4 that the boat that did not *start* is disqualified and the match is terminated.

C9 REQUESTS FOR REDRESS OR REOPENING; APPEALS; OTHER PROCEEDINGS

C9.1 There shall be no request for redress or an appeal from a decision made under rule C5, C6, C7 or C8. In rule 66 the third sentence is changed to 'A *party* to the hearing may not ask for a reopening.'

C9.2 A competitor may not base a request for redress on a claim that an action by an official boat was improper. The protest committee may decide to consider giving redress in such circumstances but only if it believes that an official boat, including an umpire boat, may have seriously interfered with a competing boat.

C9.3 No proceedings of any kind may be taken in relation to any action or non-action by the umpires, except as permitted in rule C9.2.

C10 SCORING

C10.1 The winning competitor of each match scores one point (half of one point each for a dead heat); the loser scores no points.

C10.2 When a competitor withdraws from part of an event the scores of all completed races shall stand.

C10.3 When a multiple round robin is terminated with an incomplete round robin, only one point shall be available for all the matches sailed between any two competitors, as follows:

Number of matches completed between any two competitors	*Points for each win*
1	One point
2	One-half point
3	One-third point
(etc.)	

C10.4 In a round-robin series,

(a) competitors shall be placed in order of their total scores, highest score first;

(b) a competitor who has won a match but is disqualified for breaking a *rule* against a competitor in another match shall lose the point for that match (but the losing competitor shall not be awarded the point); and

(c) the overall position between competitors who have sailed in different groups shall be decided by the highest score.

C10.5 In a knockout series the sailing instructions shall state the minimum number of points required to win a series between two competitors. When a knockout series is terminated it shall be decided in favour of the competitor with the higher score.

C11 TIES

C11.1 Round-Robin Series

A round-robin series means a grouping of competitors who all sail against each other one or more times. Each separate stage identified in the event format shall be a separate round-robin series irrespective of the number of times each competitor sails against each other competitor in that stage.

Ties between two or more competitors in a round-robin series shall be broken by the following methods, in order, until all ties are broken. When one or more ties are only partially broken, rules C11.1(a) to C11.1(e) shall be reapplied to them. Ties shall be decided in favour of the competitor(s) who

(a) placed in order, has the highest score in the matches between the tied competitors.

(b) when the tie is between two competitors in a multiple round robin, has won the last match between the two competitors.

(c) has the most points against the competitor placed highest in the round-robin series or, if necessary, second highest, and so on until the tie is broken. When two separate ties have to be resolved but the resolution of each depends upon resolving the other, the following principles shall be used in the rule C11.1(c) procedure:

(1) the higher-place tie shall be resolved before the lower-place tie, and

(2) all the competitors in the lower-place tie shall be treated as a single competitor for the purposes of rule C11.1(c).

(d) after applying rule C10.4(c), has the highest place in the different groups, irrespective of the number of competitors in each group.

(e) has the highest place in the most recent stage of the event (fleet race, round robin, etc.).

C11.2 Knockout Series

Ties (including 0–0) between two competitors in a knockout series shall be broken by the following methods, in order, until the tie is broken. The tie shall be decided in favour of the competitor who

(a) has the highest place in the most recent round-robin series, applying rule C11.1 if necessary;

(b) has won the most recent match in the event between the tied competitors.

C11.3 Remaining Ties

When rule C11.1 or C11.2 does not resolve a tie,

(a) if the tie needs to be resolved for a later stage of the event (or another event for which the event is a direct qualifier), the tie shall be broken by a sail-off when practicable. When the race committee decides a sail-off is not practicable the tie shall be broken by a draw.

(b) to decide the winner of an event that is not a direct qualifier for another event, or the overall position between competitors eliminated in one round of a knockout series, a sail-off may be used (but not a draw).

(c) when a tie is not broken any monetary prizes or ranking points for tied places shall be added together and divided equally among the tied competitors.

Note: A Standard Notice of Race and Standard Sailing Instructions for match racing are available from the ISAF.

APPENDIX D
TEAM RACING RULES

Team races shall be sailed under The Racing Rules of Sailing *as changed by this appendix. If umpires will be used the sailing instructions shall so state.*

D1 CHANGES TO THE RACING RULES

D1.1 Changes to the Rules of Part 2

(a) Rule 17.2 is changed to 'Except on a beat to windward, while a boat is less than two of her hull lengths from a *leeward* boat, she shall not sail below her *proper course* unless she gybes.'

(b) The first sentence of rule 18.2(c) is changed to 'If a boat was *clear ahead* at the time she reached the *two-length zone*, or she later became *clear ahead* when another boat passed head to wind, the boat *clear astern* shall thereafter *keep clear*.'

(c) Rule 18.4 is deleted.

(d) Add new rule 22.3: 'A boat that has *finished* shall not act to interfere with a boat that has not *finished*.'

(e) Add new rule 22.4: 'When boats in different races meet, any change of course by either boat shall be consistent with complying with a *rule* or trying to win her own race.'

D1.2 Other Additional Rules

(a) There shall be no penalty for breaking a rule of Part 2 when the incident is between boats on the same team and there is no contact.

(b) Add to rule 41: 'However, a boat may receive help from another boat on her team provided electronic communication is not used.'

(c) A boat is not eligible for redress based on damage or injury caused by another boat on her team.

D2 PROTESTS AND PENALTIES

D2.1 Protests and Exoneration

(a) The third sentence of rule 61.1(a) and all of rule 61.1(a)(2) are deleted.

(b) A boat that, while *racing*, may have broken a rule of Part 2 (except rule 14 when she has caused damage or injury) or rule 42 may take a penalty complying with rule 44.2, except that only one turn is required.

(c) The sailing instructions may state that rule D2.4(b) applies to all *protests*.

D2.2 Umpired Races

Races to be umpired shall be identified either in the sailing instructions or by the display of flag U no later than the warning signal.

(a) When a boat protests under a rule of Part 2 or under rule 31.1, 42 or 44, she is not entitled to a hearing, except under rule 14 when there is damage or injury. Instead, when the protested boat fails either to acknowledge breaking a *rule* or to take the appropriate penalty, the protesting boat may request a decision by conspicuously displaying a yellow flag and hailing 'Umpire'.

(b) An umpire shall signal a decision as follows:

(1) A green flag or a green and white flag means 'No penalty'.

(2) A red flag means 'One or more boats are penalized.' The umpire shall hail or signal to identify each boat to be penalized.

(c) A boat penalized under rule D2.2(b)(2) shall take a Two-Turns Penalty under rule 44.2.

(d) PENALTIES INITIATED BY UMPIRES

When a boat

(1) breaks rule 31.1 or 42, or a rule of Part 2 through contact with another boat on her team, and does not take a penalty;

(2) fails to comply with rule D2.2(c);

(3) commits a breach of sportsmanship; or

(4) breaks rule 14 when damage or injury may have been caused;

or when a boat or her team gains an advantage despite taking a penalty, an umpire may take action without a *protest* from another boat. The umpire may impose a penalty of one or more turns, each including one tack and one gybe, signalled by displaying a red flag and hailing the boat accordingly, or report the incident to the protest committee, signalled by displaying a black flag, or both.

D2.3 Alternative Umpiring Rules

Each of these rules applies only if the sailing instructions so state.

(a) SINGLE-FLAG PROTEST PROCEDURE

Rule D2.2(a) is replaced by

> When a boat protests under a rule of Part 2 or under rule 31.1, 42 or 44, she is not entitled to a hearing, except under rule 14 when there is damage or injury. Instead, a boat involved in the incident may promptly acknowledge breaking a *rule* and take the appropriate penalty. If no boat takes a penalty, an umpire shall decide whether any boat has broken a *rule*, and shall signal the decision in compliance with rule D2.2(b).

(b) RACES WITH LIMITED UMPIRING

> Rule D2.2 applies, except that when a boat complies with rule D2.2(a) and either there is no decision signalled or an umpire displays a yellow flag signalling he has insufficient facts to decide, the protesting boat is entitled to a hearing.

D2.4 Additional Protest and Redress Rules When Races Are Umpired

(a) Neither the race committee nor the protest committee shall protest a boat for breaking a rule listed in rule D2.2(a), except under rule 14 when there is damage or injury.

(b) Protests and requests for redress need not be in writing. The protest committee may take evidence in any way it considers appropriate and may communicate its decision orally.

(c) There shall be no request for redress or appeal by a boat arising from a decision, action or non-action by an umpire. The protest committee may decide to consider giving redress when it believes that an official boat, including an umpire boat, may have seriously interfered with a competing boat.

D3 SCORING A RACE

D3.1 (a) Each boat *finishing* a race, whether or not rule 28.1 has been complied with, shall be scored points equal to her finishing place. All other boats shall be scored points equal to the number of boats entitled to *race*.

(b) In addition, a boat's points shall be increased as follows:

Rule broken	*Penalty points*
Rule 28.1 when as a result she or her team has gained an advantage	10
Any other *rule* broken while *racing* for which a penalty has not been taken	6

(c) After a hearing the protest committee may penalize as follows:

(1) When a boat has broken a *rule* and as a result her team has gained an advantage, it may increase that boat's points.

(2) When a boat has broken rule 1 or 2, rule 14 when she has caused damage or injury, or a *rule* when not *racing*, it may penalize the boat's team by half or more race wins, or it may impose no penalty.

(d) The team with the lower total points wins the race. If the totals are equal, the team that did not have the first-place boat wins.

D3.2 When all boats on one team have *finished*, retired or failed to *start*, the race committee may stop the race. The other team's boats *racing* at that time shall be scored the points they would have received had they *finished*.

D4 SCORING A SERIES

D4.1 When two or more teams are competing in a series, the winner shall be the team scoring the greatest number of race wins. The other teams shall be ranked in order of number of race wins.

D4.2 When necessary, ties in a completed series shall be broken using, in order,

(a) the number of races won when the tied teams met;

(b) the points scored when the tied teams met;

(c) if two teams remain tied, the last race between them;

(d) total points scored in all races against common opponents;

(e) a sail-off if possible, otherwise a game of chance.

If a multiple tie is only partially resolved by one of these, then the remaining tie shall be broken by starting again at rule D4.2(a).

D4.3 If a series is not completed, teams shall be ranked according to the results from completed rounds, and ties shall be broken whenever possible using the results from races between the tied teams in the incomplete round. If no round has been completed, teams shall be ranked in order of their percentages of races won. Other ties shall be broken as provided in rule D4.2.

D5 BREAKDOWNS WHEN BOATS ARE SUPPLIED BY THE ORGANIZING AUTHORITY

D5.1 A supplied boat suffering a breakdown, and seeking redress as a result, shall display a red flag at the first reasonable opportunity and, if possible, continue *racing*. The race committee shall decide redress as provided in rules D5.2 and D5.3.

D5.2 When the race committee decides that the boat's finishing position was made significantly worse, that the breakdown was through no fault of the crew, and that in the same circumstances a reasonably competent crew would not have been able to avoid the breakdown, it shall make as equitable a decision as possible. This may be to order the race to be resailed or, when the boat's finishing position was predictable, award her points for that position. Any doubt about a boat's position when she broke down shall be resolved against her.

D5.3 A breakdown caused by defective supplied equipment or a breach of a *rule* by an opponent shall not normally be determined to be the fault of the crew, but one caused by careless handling, capsizing or a breach by a boat on the same team shall be. Any doubt about the fault of the crew shall be resolved in the boat's favour.

APPENDIX E
RADIO-CONTROLLED BOAT RACING RULES

Races for radio-controlled boats shall be sailed under The Racing Rules of Sailing *as changed by this appendix*

E1 TERMINOLOGY, RACE SIGNALS, DEFINITIONS AND FUNDAMENTAL RULES

E1.1 Terminology

'Boat' means a boat that is radio-controlled by a competitor who is not on board. For 'race' used as a noun outside this appendix and outside Appendix A read 'heat'. Within this appendix, a race consists of one or more heats and is completed when the last heat in the race is finished. An 'event' consists of one or more races. A 'series' consists of a specified number of races or events.

E1.2 Race Signals

Delete Race Signals. All signals shall be made orally or by other sounds described in this appendix or the sailing instructions.

E1.3 Definitions

(a) Add to the definition *Interested Party*: 'but not a competitor when acting as an observer'.

(b) Delete the definition *Two-Length Zone* and add a new definition, *Four-Length Zone:* 'The area around a *mark* or *obstruction* within a distance of four hull lengths of the boat nearer to it.' Wherever *'two-length zone'* is used in rule 18 replace it with *'four-length zone'*.

E1.4 Personal Buoyancy

Rule 1.2 is changed to 'When on board a rescue boat, each competitor shall be responsible for wearing personal buoyancy adequate for the conditions.'

E1.5 Aerials

Transmitter aerial extremities shall be adequately protected. When a protest committee finds that a competitor has broken this rule it shall either warn him and give him time to comply or penalize him.

E2 PART 2 - WHEN BOATS MEET

Rule 21 is changed to

CAPSIZED OR ENTANGLED

If possible, a boat shall avoid a boat that is capsized or entangled, or has not regained control after capsizing or entanglement. A boat is capsized when her masthead is in the water. Two or more boats are entangled when lying together for a period of time so that no boat is capable of manoeuvring to break free of the other(s).

E3 PART 3 - CONDUCT OF A RACE

E3.1 Races with Observers

The race committee may appoint race observers, who may be competitors. They shall remain in the control area while boats are *racing* and they shall hail and repeat the identity of boats that contact a *mark* or another boat. Such hails shall be made from the control area. Observers shall report all unresolved incidents to the race committee at the end of the heat.

E3.2 Course Board

Rule J2.1(4) is deleted. A course board showing the course and the limits of the control area and launching area(s) shall be located next to or within the control area with information clearly visible to competitors while *racing*.

E3.3 Control and Launching Areas

The control and launching area(s) shall be defined by the sailing instructions. Competitors *racing* shall remain in the control area while a heat is in progress, except that competitors may briefly go to and return from the launching area to perform functions permitted in rule E4.5. Competitors not *racing* shall remain outside the control and launching areas except when offering assistance under rule E4.2 or when acting as race observers.

E3.4 Non-applicable Rules

Delete the second sentence of rule 25 and all of rule 33.

E3.5 Starting Races

Rule 26 is changed to

> Audible signals for starting a heat shall be at one-minute intervals and shall be a warning signal, a preparatory signal and a starting signal. During the minute before the starting signal, oral signals shall be made at ten-second intervals, and during the final ten seconds at one-second intervals. Each signal shall be timed from the beginning of its sound.

E3.6 Starting Penalties

In rules 29.1 and 30 delete the word 'crew'. Throughout rule 30 oral announcements shall be used instead of flag signals.

E3.7 Starting and Finishing Lines

The starting and finishing lines shall be tangential to, and on the course side of, the starting and finishing *marks*.

E3.8 Individual Recall

In rule 29.1 replace all after 'the race committee shall promptly' with 'twice hail "Recall (sail numbers)"'.

E3.9 General Recall

In rule 29.2 replace all after 'the race committee may' with 'twice hail "General recall" and make two loud sounds'. The warning signal for a new start for the recalled class shall be made shortly thereafter, and the starts for any succeeding classes shall follow the new start.

E3.10 Shortening or Abandoning after the Start

In rule 32.1(b) replace 'foul weather' with 'thunderstorms'. Delete rule 32.1(c).

E4 PART 4 - OTHER REQUIREMENTS WHEN RACING

E4.1 Non-applicable rules

Rules 43, 47, 48, 49, 50, 52 and 54 are deleted.

E4.2 Outside Help

Rule 41 is changed to

(a) A competitor shall not give tactical or strategic advice to a competitor who is racing.

(b) A competitor who is *racing* shall not receive outside help except

(1) A boat that has gone ashore or aground outside the launching area, or become entangled with another boat or a *mark*, may be freed and relaunched only with outside help from a rescue boat crew.

(2) Competitors who are not *racing* and others may give outside help in the launching area as permitted by rule E4.5.

E4.3 Propulsion

Rule 42 is changed so that any reference to body movement is deleted. Rule 42.3(f) is also deleted.

E4.4 Penalties for Breaking Rules of Part 2

Throughout rule 44 the penalty shall be one turn, including one tack and one gybe.

E4.5 Launching and Relaunching

Rule 45 is changed to

(a) A boat scheduled to *race* in a heat may be launched, held on the bank, taken ashore or relaunched at any time during the heat. However, she shall not be released between the preparatory and starting signals.

(b) Boats shall be launched or recovered only from within a launching area, except as provided in rule E4.2(b)(1).

(c) While ashore or within a launching area, boats may be adjusted, drained of water or repaired; have their sails changed or reefed; have entangled objects removed; or have radio equipment repaired or changed.

E4.6 Person in Charge

In rule 46 replace 'have on board' with 'be radio-controlled by'.

E4.7 Radio

(a) A competitor shall not transmit radio signals that cause interference with the radio reception of other boats.

(b) A competitor found to have broken rule E4.7(a) shall not race until he has proven compliance with that rule.

E4.9 Boat Out of Radio Control

A competitor who loses radio control of his boat shall promptly hail and repeat '(The boat's sail number) out of control'. Such a boat shall be considered to have retired and shall thereafter be an *obstruction*.

E5 PART 5 PROTESTS, REDRESS, HEARINGS, MISCONDUCT AND APPEALS

E5.1 Right to Protest; Right to Request Redress or Rule 69 Action

Add to rule 60.1(a): 'A *protest* alleging a breach of a rule of Part 2, 3 or 4 shall be made only by a competitor within the control or launching area and by a boat scheduled to *race* in the heat in which the incident occurred.'

E5.2 Informing the Protestee

In rule 61.1(a) replace all after the first sentence with 'When her *protest* concerns an incident in the racing area that she is involved in or sees, she shall twice hail "(Her own sail number) protest (the sail number of the other boat)".'

E5.3 Protest Time Limit

In rule 61.3 replace 'two hours' with '15 minutes' and add: 'A boat intending to protest shall also inform the race committee within five minutes of the end of the relevant heat.'

E5.4 Accepting Responsibility

A boat that acknowledges breaking a rule of Part 2, 3 or 4 before the *protest* is found to be valid may retire from the relevant heat without further penalty.

E5.5 Redress

(a) Add to rule 62.1:

(e) radio interference, or

(f) an entanglement or grounding because of the action of a boat that was breaking a rule of Part 2 or of a vessel not *racing* that was required to keep clear.

(b) In rule 62.2 replace 'two hours' with '15 minutes'.

E5.6 Right to Be Present

In rule 63.3(a) replace 'shall have been on board' with 'shall have been radio-controlling them'.

E5.7 Taking Evidence and Finding Facts

Add to rule 63.6: 'Evidence about an alleged breach of a rule of Part 2, 3 or 4 given by competitors shall be accepted only from a competitor who was within the control or launching area and whose boat was scheduled to *race* in the heat in which the incident occurred.'

E5.8 Penalties and Exoneration

When a protest committee finds that a boat has broken rule E3.3, E4.2(a) or E4.5, it shall either disqualify her from her next race or require her to make one or more penalty turns in her next race as soon as possible after *starting*.

E5.9 Decision on Redress

Add to rule 64.2: 'If a boat given redress was damaged, she shall be given reasonable time, but not more than 30 minutes, to effect repairs before her next heat.'

E5.10 Reopening a Hearing

In rule 66 replace '24 hours' with 'ten minutes'.

E6 APPENDIX G IDENTIFICATION ON SAILS

Appendix G is changed as follows:

(a) The text of rule G1.1 before rule G1.1(a) is changed to

> Every boat of an ISAF Radio Sailing Division (RSD) class shall display a sail number on both sides of each sail. Class insignia and national letters shall be displayed on mainsails as stated in rules G1.1(a), G1.1(b) and E6(f)(1).

(b) Rule G1.1(c) is changed to

> a sail number, which shall be the last two digits of the boat registration number or the competitor's personal number allotted by the relevant issuing authority. A single-digit number shall be prefixed with a '0'. There shall be space in front of a sail number for the prefix '1', which may be required by the race committee where there is a conflict between sail numbers. Where a conflict remains, the race committee shall require that sail numbers be suitably changed until the conflict is resolved. Any prefix '1' or other required change shall become part of the sail number.

(c) Delete the sentence after rule G1.1(c).

(d) Rule G1.2(b) is changed to

> The height of characters and distance between them on the same and opposite sides of the sail shall be as follows:

	Minimum	Maximum
Class insignia:		
Except where positioned back to back, shortest distance between insignia on opposite sides of sail	20mm	
Sail numbers:		
Height of characters	100mm	110mm
Shortest distance between adjoining characters on same side of sail	20mm	30mm
Shortest distance between sail numbers on opposite sides of sail and between sail numbers and other identification	60mm	
National letters:		
Height of characters	60mm	70mm
Shortest distance between adjoining characters on same side of sail	13mm	23mm
Shortest distance between national letters on opposite sides of sail	40mm	

(e) Rule G1.3 is changed to

(1) Class insignia may be positioned back to back on opposite sides of the sail where the design coincides. Otherwise class insignia, sail numbers and national letters shall be positioned at different heights, with those on the starboard side being uppermost.

(2) On a mainsail, sail numbers shall be positioned above the national letters and below the class insignia.

(3) Sail numbers shall be positioned on a mainsail above the line perpendicular to the luff through the quarter leech point.

(f) Where the size of a sail makes it impossible to comply with the minimum dimensions in rule E6(d) or the positioning requirements in rule E6(e)(3), exceptions are permitted in the following order of priority:

(1) omission of national letters;

(2) position of the mainsail sail numbers lower than the line perpendicular to the luff through the quarter leech point;

(3) reduction of the shortest distance between sail numbers on opposite sides of the sail provided the shortest distance is not less than 20 mm;

(4) reduction of the height of sail numbers.

APPENDIX F
APPEALS PROCEDURES

See rule 70. A national authority may change this appendix by prescription but it shall not be changed by sailing instructions.

F1 APPEALS AND REQUESTS

Appeals, requests by protest committees for confirmation or correction of their decisions, and requests for interpretations of the *rules* shall be made to the national authority of the venue.

F2 SUBMISSION OF DOCUMENTS

RYA F2.1 Within 15 days of receiving the protest committee's written decision or its decision not to reopen a hearing, the appellant shall send an appeal and a copy of the protest committee's decision to the national authority. The appeal shall state why the appellant believes the protest committee's decision or its procedures were incorrect.

F2.2 The appellant shall also send, with the appeal or as soon as possible thereafter, all of the following documents that are available to her:

(a) the written *protest(s)* or request(s) for redress;

(b) a diagram, prepared or endorsed by the protest committee, showing the positions and tracks of all boats involved, the course to the next *mark* and the required side, the force and direction of the wind, and, if relevant, the depth of water and direction and speed of any current;

(c) the notice of race, the sailing instructions, any other conditions governing the event, and any changes to them;

(d) any additional relevant documents; and

(e) the names, postal and e-mail addresses, and telephone numbers of all *parties* to the hearing and the protest committee chairman.

F2.3 A request from a protest committee for confirmation or correction of its decision shall be sent within 15 days of the decision and shall include the decision and the documents listed in rule F2.2. A request for an interpretation of the *rules* shall include assumed facts.

F3 RESPONSIBILITIES OF NATIONAL AUTHORITY AND PROTEST COMMITTEE

Upon receipt of an appeal or a request for confirmation or correction, the national authority shall send to the *parties* and protest committee copies of the appeal or request and the protest committee's decision. It shall ask the protest committee for any relevant documents listed in rule F2.2 not sent by the appellant or the protest committee, and the protest committee shall promptly send them to the national authority. When the national authority has received them it shall send copies to the *parties*.

RYA F4 COMMENTS

The *parties* and protest committee may make comments on the appeal or request or on any of the documents listed in rule F2.2 by sending them in writing to the national authority. Comments on any document shall be made within 15 days of receiving it from the national authority. The national authority shall send copies of the comments to the *parties* and protest committee as appropriate.

F5 INADEQUATE FACTS; REOPENING

The national authority shall accept the protest committee's finding of facts except when it decides they are inadequate. In that case it shall require the committee to provide additional facts or other information, or to reopen the hearing and report any new finding of facts, and the committee shall promptly do so.

F6 WITHDRAWING AN APPEAL

An appellant may withdraw an appeal before it is decided by accepting the protest committee's decision.

APPENDIX G
IDENTIFICATION ON SAILS

See rule 77.

RYA G1 ISAF INTERNATIONAL CLASS BOATS

G1.1 Identification

Every boat of an ISAF International Class or Recognized Class shall carry on her mainsail and, as provided in rules G1.3(d) and G1.3(e) for letters and numbers only, on her spinnaker and headsail

(a) the insignia denoting her class;

(b) at all international events, except when the boats are provided to all competitors, national letters denoting her national authority from the table below. For the purposes of this rule, international events are ISAF events, world and continental championships, and events described as international events in their notices of race and sailing instructions; and

(c) a sail number of no more than four digits allotted by her national authority or, when so required by the class rules, by the international class association. The four-digit limitation does not apply to classes whose ISAF membership or recognition took effect before 1 April 1997. Alternatively, if permitted in the class rules, an owner may be allotted a personal sail number by the relevant issuing authority, which may be used on all his boats in that class.

Sails measured before 31 March 1999 shall comply with rule G1.1 or with the rules applicable at the time of measurement.

NATIONAL SAIL LETTERS

National authority	*Letters*
Algeria	ALG
American Samoa	ASA
Andorra	AND
Angola	ANG
Antigua	ANT
Argentina	ARG
Australia	AUS
Austria	AUT

National authority	*Letters*
Azerbaijan	AZE
Bahamas	BAH
Bahrain	BRN
Barbados	BAR
Belarus	BLR
Belgium	BEL
Bermuda	BER
Brazil	BRA
British Virgin Islands	IVB
Bulgaria	BUL
Canada	CAN
Cayman Islands	CAY
Chile	CHI
China, PR	CHN
Chinese Taipei	TPE
Columbia	COL
Cook Islands	COK
Croatia	CRO
Cuba	CUB
Cyprus	CYP
Czech Republic	CZE
Denmark	DEN
Dominican Republic	DOM
Ecuador	ECU
Egypt	EGY
El Salvador	ESA
Estonia	EST
Fiji	FIJ
Finland	FIN
France	FRA
FYRO Macedonia	MKD
Germany	GER
Great Britain	GBR
Greece	GRE
Grenada	GRN
Guam	GUM
Guatemala	GUA
Hong Kong	HKG
Hungary	HUN
Iceland	ISL

National authority	*Letters*
India	IND
Indonesia	INA
Ireland	IRL
Israel	ISR
Italy	ITA
Jamaica	JAM
Japan	JPN
Kazakhstan	KAZ
Kenya	KEN
Korea	KOR
Kuwait	KUW
Latvia	LAT
Lebanon	LIB
Libya	LBA
Liechtenstein	LIE
Lithuania	LTU
Luxembourg	LUX
Malaysia	MAS
Malta	MLT
Mauritius	MRI
Mexico	MEX
Micronesia	FSM
Moldova	MDA
Monaco	MON
Morocco	MAR
Myanmar	MYA
Namibia	NAM
The Netherlands	NED
Netherlands Antilles	AHO
New Zealand	NZL
Norway	NOR
Pakistan	PAK
Papua New Guinea	PNG
Paraguay	PAR
Peru	PER
Philippines	PHI
Poland	POL
Portugal	POR
Puerto Rico	PUR
Qatar	QAT

National authority	*Letters*	*National authority*	*Letters*
Romania	ROM	Tahiti	TAH
Russia	RUS	Thailand	THA
Samoa	SAM	Trinidad & Tobago	TRI
San Marino	SMR	Tunisia	TUN
Seychelles	SEY	Turkey	TUR
Singapore	SIN	Ukraine	UKR
Slovak Republic	SVK	United Arab Emirates	UAE
Slovenia	SLO	United States of America	USA
Solomon Islands	SOL	Uruguay	URU
South Africa	RSA	US Virgin Islands	ISV
Spain	ESP	Venezuela	VEN
Sri Lanka	SRI	Yugoslavia	YUG
St Lucia	LCA	Zimbabwe	ZIM
Sweden	SWE		
Switzerland	SUI		

G1.2 Specifications

(a) National letters and sail numbers shall be in capital letters and Arabic numerals, clearly legible and of the same colour. Commercially available typefaces giving the same or better legibility than Helvetica are acceptable.

(b) The height of characters and space between adjoining characters on the same and opposite sides of the sail shall be related to the boat's overall length as follows:

Overall length	*Minimum height*	*Minimum space between characters and from edge of sail*
under 3.5m	230mm	45mm
3.5 m - 8.5m	300mm	60mm
8.5 m - 11m	375mm	75mm
over 11m	450mm	90mm

G1.3 Positioning

Class insignia, national letters and sail numbers shall be positioned as follows:

(a) Except as provided in rules G1.3(d) and G1.3(e), class insignia, national letters and sail numbers shall when possible be wholly above an arc whose centre is the head point and whose radius is 60% of the leech length. They shall be placed at different heights on the two sides of the sail, those on the starboard side being uppermost.

(b) The class insignia shall be placed above the national letters. If the class insignia is of such a design that two of them coincide when placed back to back on both sides of the sail, they may be so placed.

(c) National letters shall be placed above the sail number.

(d) The national letters and sail number shall be displayed on the front side of a spinnaker but may be placed on both sides. They shall be displayed wholly below an arc whose centre is the head point and whose radius is 40% of the foot median and, when possible, wholly above an arc whose radius is 60% of the foot median.

(e) The national letters and sail number shall be displayed on both sides of a headsail whose clew can extend behind the mast 30% or more of the mainsail foot length. They shall be displayed wholly below an arc whose centre is the head point and whose radius is half the luff length and, if possible, wholly above an arc whose radius is 75% of the luff length.

RYA G2 OTHER BOATS

Other boats shall comply with the rules of their national authority or class association in regard to the allotment, carrying and size of insignia, letters and numbers. Such rules shall, when practicable, conform to the above requirements.

G3 CHARTERED OR LOANED BOATS

When so stated in the notice of race or sailing instructions, a boat chartered or loaned for an event may carry national letters or a sail number in contravention of her class rules.

G4 WARNINGS AND PENALTIES

When a protest committee finds that a boat has broken a rule of this appendix it shall either warn her and give her time to comply or penalize her.

G5 CHANGES BY CLASS RULES

ISAF classes may change the rules of this appendix provided the changes have first been approved by the ISAF.

APPENDIX H
WEIGHING CLOTHING AND EQUIPMENT

See rule 43. This appendix shall not be changed by sailing instructions or prescriptions of national authorities.

H1 Items of clothing and equipment to be weighed shall be arranged on a rack. After being saturated in water the items shall be allowed to drain freely for one minute before being weighed. The rack must allow the items to hang as they would hang from clothes hangers, so as to allow the water to drain freely. Pockets that have drain-holes that cannot be closed shall be empty, but pockets or items that can hold water shall be full.

H2 When the weight recorded exceeds the amount permitted, the competitor may rearrange the items on the rack and the measurer shall again soak and weigh them. This procedure may be repeated a second time if the weight still exceeds the amount permitted.

H3 A competitor wearing a dry-suit may choose an alternative means of weighing the items.

(a) The dry-suit and items of clothing and equipment that are worn outside the dry-suit shall be weighed as described above.

(b) Clothing worn underneath the dry-suit shall be weighed as worn while racing, without draining.

(c) The two weights shall be added together.

APPENDIX J
NOTICE OF RACE AND SAILING INSTRUCTIONS

See rules 88.2(a) and 89.2. The term 'race' includes a regatta or other series of races.

J1 NOTICE OF RACE CONTENTS

J1.1 The notice of race shall include the following information:

(1) the title, place and dates of the race and name of the organizing authority;

(2) that the race will be governed by the *rules* as defined in The *Racing Rules of Sailing*;

(3) a list of any other documents that will govern the event (for example, *The Equipment Rules of Sailing*, to the extent that they apply), stating where or how each document or a copy of it may be seen;

(4) the classes to race, any handicap or rating system that will be used and the classes to which it will apply, conditions of entry and any restrictions on entries;

(5) the times of registration and warning signals for the practice race or first race, and succeeding races if known.

J1.2 The notice of race shall include any of the following that would help competitors decide whether to attend the event or that conveys other information they will need before the sailing instructions become available:

(1) identification of any racing rules that will be changed, a summary of the changes, and a statement that the changes will appear in full in the sailing instructions (see rule 86);

(2) that advertising will be restricted to Category A (see ISAF Regulation 20) and other information related to Regulation 20;

(3) that the ISAF Sailor Classification Code will apply;

(4) for an international event, any prescriptions of the national authority that may require advance preparation;

(5) the procedure for advance registration or entry, including fees and any closing dates;

(6) an entry form, to be signed by the boat's owner or owner's representative, containing words such as 'I agree to be bound by *The Racing Rules of Sailing* and by all other rules that govern this event';

(7) measurement procedures or requirements for measurement or rating certificates;

(8) the time and place at which the sailing instructions will be available;

(9) any changes to class rules, referring specifically to each rule and stating the change;

(10) the courses to be sailed;

(11) the penalty for breaking a rule of Part 2, other than the Two-Turns Penalty;

(12) denial of the right of appeal, subject to rule 70.4;

(13) the scoring system, if different from the Low Point System in Appendix A, the number of races scheduled and the minimum number that must be completed to constitute a series;

(14) prizes.

J2 SAILING INSTRUCTION CONTENTS

J2.1 The sailing instructions shall include the following information:

(1) that the race will be governed by the *rules* as defined in *The Racing Rules of Sailing*;

(2) a list of any other documents that will govern the event (for example, *The Equipment Rules of Sailing*, to the extent that they apply);

(3) the schedule of races, the classes to race and times of warning signals for each class;

(4) the course(s) to be sailed, or a list of *marks* from which the course will be selected and, if relevant, how courses will be signalled;

(5) descriptions of *marks*, including starting and finishing *marks*, stating the order and side on which each is to be left and identifying all rounding *marks* (see rule 28.1);

(6) descriptions of the starting and finishing lines, class flags and any special signals to be used;

(7) the time limit, if any, for *finishing*;

(8) the handicap or rating system to be used, if any, and the classes to which it will apply;

(9) the scoring system, included by reference to Appendix A, to class rules or other *rules* governing the event, or stated in full. State the number of races scheduled and the minimum number that must be completed to constitute a series.

J2.2 The sailing instructions shall include those of the following that will apply:

(1) that advertising will be restricted to Category A (see ISAF Regulation 20) and other information related to Regulation 20;

(2) that the ISAF Sailor Classification Code will apply;

(3) replacement of the relevant rules of Part 2 with the *International Regulations for Preventing Collisions at Sea* or other government right-of-way rules, the time(s) or place(s) they will apply, and any night signals to be used by the race committee;

(4) changes to the racing rules permitted by rule 86, referring specifically to each rule and stating the change (if rule 86.2 applies, state the authorization);

(5) changes to the prescriptions of the national authority (see rule 87);

(6) at an international event, a copy in English of the prescriptions of the national authority that will apply;

(7) changes to class rules, referring specifically to each rule and stating the change;

(8) restrictions controlling changes to boats when supplied by the organizing authority;

(9) the registration procedure;

(10) measurement or inspection procedure;

(11) location(s) of official notice board(s);

(12) procedure for changing the sailing instructions;

(13) safety requirements, such as requirements and signals for personal buoyancy, check-in at the starting area, and check-out and check-in ashore;

(14) declaration requirements;

(15) signals to be made ashore and location of signal station(s);

(16) the racing area (a chart is recommended);

(17) approximate course length and approximate length of windward legs;

(18) description of any area designated by the race committee to be an *obstruction* (see the definition *Obstruction*);

(19) the time limit, if any, for boats other than the first boat to *finish*;

(20) time allowances;

(21) the location of the starting area and any applicable restrictions;

(22) any special procedures or signals for individual or general recall;

(23) boats identifying *mark* locations;

(24) any special procedures or signals for changing the position of a *mark* after the start;

(25) any special procedures for shortening the course or for *finishing* a shortened course;

(26) restrictions on use of support boats, plastic pools, radios, etc.; on hauling out; and on outside assistance provided to a boat that is not *racing*;

(27) the penalty for breaking a rule of Part 2, other than the Two-Turns Penalty;

(28) penalization without a hearing under rule 67 for breaking rule 42;

(29) whether Appendix P will apply;

(30) protest procedure and times and place of hearings;

(31) if rule N1.4(b) will apply, the time limit for requesting a hearing under that rule;

(32) denial of the right of appeal, subject to rule 70.4;

(33) the national authority's approval of the appointment of an international jury under rule 90(b);

(34) substitution of competitors;

(35) the minimum number of boats appearing in the starting area required for a race to be started;

(36) when and where races *postponed* or *abandoned* for the day will be resailed;

(37) tides and currents;

(38) prizes;

(39) other commitments of the race committee and obligations of boats.

ADDENDUM A (RYA)

The following clauses are recommended for inclusion in the Notice of Race. Before using the clauses you are advised to read Race, Training and Event Management - The Legal Aspects (G6) published by the RYA. This booklet contains much valuable advice on the subject.

While these clauses are suitable for many events, you should consider most carefully whether they are right for yours and whether there are other clauses contained in the booklet which should also be included.

1 A boat is entirely responsible for her own safety, whether afloat or ashore, and nothing, whether in the Notice of Race or Sailing Instructions or anywhere else, reduces this responsibility.

2 It is for the boat to decide whether she is fit to sail in the conditions in which she will find herself. By launching or going to sea, the boat confirms that she is fit for those conditions and her crew is competent to sail and compete in them.

3 The boat is required to hold adequate insurance and in particular to hold insurance against third party claims in the sum of at least £#.

4 Nothing done by the organisers can reduce the responsibility of the boat nor will it make the organisers responsible for any loss, damage, death or personal injury, however it may have occurred, as a result of the boat taking part in the racing. The organisers encompass everyone helping to run the race and the event, and include the organising authority, the race committee, the race officer, patrol boats and beachmasters.

5 The provision of patrol boats does not relieve the boat of her responsibilities.

Addition for offshore races

6 The boat is responsible to ensure that she is equipped and seaworthy so as to be able to face extremes of weather; that there is a crew sufficient in number, experience and fitness to withstand such weather; and that the safety equipment is properly maintained, stowed and in date and that the crew know how to use it.

Addition where boats are checked

7 The fact that the race committee conducts inspections of a boat does not reduce the responsibilities of the boat set out in this paragraph.

Declaration to be contained in the entry form immediately above the signature of the competitors

I agree to be bound by the Racing Rules of Sailing and all other rules that govern this event. In particular I have read Paragraph # of the Notice of Race and confirm that I agree to its provisions and that my boat will conform to its requirements throughout the event.

APPENDIX K
NOTICE OF RACE GUIDE

This guide provides a notice of race designed primarily for major championship regattas for one or more classes. It therefore will be particularly useful for world, continental and national championships and other events of similar importance. It can be downloaded from the ISAF website (www.sailing.org) as a basic text for producing a notice of race for any particular event.

The guide can also be useful for other events. However, for such events some of the paragraphs will be unnecessary or undesirable. Organizing authorities should therefore be careful in making their choices.

This guide relates closely to Appendix L, Sailing Instructions Guide, and its extended version Appendix LE on the ISAF website, the introduction to which contains principles that also apply to a notice of race.

To use this guide, first review rule J1 and decide which paragraphs will be needed. Paragraphs that are required by rule J1.1 are marked with an asterisk (*). Delete all inapplicable or unnecessary paragraphs. Select the version preferred where there is a choice. Follow the directions in the left margin to fill in the spaces where a solid line (_____) appears and select the preferred wording if a choice or option is shown in brackets ([. . .]).

After deleting unused paragraphs, renumber all paragraphs in sequential order. Be sure that paragraph numbers are correct where one paragraph refers to another.

The items listed below, when applicable, should be distributed with the notice of race, but should not be included as numbered paragraphs within the notice.

1 *An entry form, to be signed by the boat's owner or owner's representative, containing words such as 'I agree to be bound by* The Racing Rules of Sailing *and by all other rules that govern this event.'*

2 *In an international event, the applicable prescriptions of the national authority in English.*

3 *List of sponsors, if appropriate.*

4 *Lodging and camping information.*

5 *Description of meal facilities.*

6 *Race committee and [protest committee] [jury] members.*

7 *Special mooring or storage requirements.*

8 *Sail and boat repair facilities and ship's chandlers.*

9 *Charter boat availability.*

On separate lines, insert the full name of the regatta, the inclusive dates from measurement or the practice race until the final race or closing ceremony, the name of the organizing authority, and the city and country.

____

____

____

____

____

NOTICE OF RACE

1 RULES

1.1* The regatta will be governed by the rules as defined in *The Racing Rules of Sailing*.

Insert the name. List by number and title the prescriptions that will apply. If the second sentence is used, state the relevant prescriptions in full.

1.2 The following prescriptions of the _____ national authority will apply [and will be stated in full in the sailing instructions]. [Of these, those that may require advance preparation are stated in full below.]

(OR)

Use only if the national authority for the venue of the event has not adopted a prescription to rule 87.

1.2 No national authority prescriptions will apply.

List by name any other documents that govern the event; for example, The Equipment Rules of Sailing, *to the extent that they apply.*

1.3* _____ will apply.

See rule 86. Insert the rule number(s) and summarize the changes.

1.4 Racing rule(s) _____ will be changed as follows: _____. The changes will appear in full in the sailing instructions.

Inform competitors of proper changes. Insert the rule number(s) and class name. Make a separate statement for the rules of each class.

1.5 Rule(s) _____ of the _____ class rules [will not apply] [is (are) changed as follows: _____].

1.6 If there is a conflict between languages the English text will take precedence.

2 ADVERTISING

See ISAF Regulation 20. Include other applicable information related to Regulation 20.

Advertising will be restricted to Category A.

3* ELIGIBILITY AND ENTRY

Insert the class(es).

3.1 The regatta is open to all boats of the _____ class(es).

(OR)

Insert the class(es) and eligibility requirements.

3.1 The regatta is open to boats of the _____ class(es) that _____.

Insert the postal, fax and e-mail addresses and entry closing date.	3.2	Eligible boats may enter by completing the attached form and sending it, together with the required fee, to _____ by _____.
Insert any conditions	3.3	Late entries will be accepted under the following conditions: _____.
Insert any restrictions.	3.4	The following restrictions on the number of boats apply: _____.

4 CLASSIFICATION

The ISAF Sailor Classification Code will apply.

5 FEES

Insert all required fees for racing..

5.1 Required fees are as follows:

Class	*Fee*
_____	_____
_____	_____
_____	_____

Insert optional fees (e.g. for social events).

5.2 Other fees:

_____

_____

6 QUALIFYING SERIES AND FINAL SERIES

Use only when a class is divided into fleets racing a qualifying series and a final series.

The regatta will consist of a qualifying series and a final series.

7 SCHEDULE

Insert the day, date and times..

7.1* Registration:
Day and date _____
From _____ To _____

Insert the day, date and times.

7.2 Measurement and inspection:
Day and date _____
From _____ To _____

Revise as desired and insert the dates and classes. Include a practice race if any. When the series consists of qualifying races and final races, specify them. The schedule can also be given in an attachment..

7.3* Dates of racing:

Date	Class _____	Class _____
_____	racing	racing
_____	racing	reserve day
_____	reserve day	racing
_____	racing	racing
_____	racing	racing

Insert the classes and numbers.

7.4 Number of races:

Class	*Number*	*Races per day*
_____	_____	_____
_____	_____	_____

Insert the time.

7.5* The scheduled time of the warning signal for the [practice race] [first race] [each day] is _____.

8 MEASUREMENTS

Each boat shall produce a valid [measurement] [rating] certificate.

(OR)

List the measurements with appropriate references to the class rules.

Each boat shall produce a valid [measurement] [rating] certificate. In addition the following measurements [may] [will] be taken: _____.

9 SAILING INSTRUCTIONS

Insert the time, date and location.

The sailing instructions will be available after _____ on _____ at _____.

10 VENUE

Insert a number or letter. Provide a marked map with driving instructions.

10.1 Attachment _____ shows the location of the regatta harbour.

Insert a number or letter. Provide a marked map or chart.

10.2 Attachment _____ shows the location of the racing areas.

11 THE COURSES

Include the description.

The courses to be sailed will be as follows: _____.

(OR)

Insert a number or letter. A method of illustrating various courses is shown in Addendum A of Appendix L or LE. Insert the course length if applicable.

The diagrams in Attachment _____ show the courses, including the approximate angles between legs, the order in which marks are to be passed, and the side on which each mark is to be left. [The approximate course length will be _____.]

12 PENALTY SYSTEM

Include paragraph 12.1 only when the Two-Turns Penalty will not be used. Insert the number of places or describe the penalties.

12.1 The Scoring Penalty, rule 44.3, will apply. The penalty will be _____ places.

(OR)

12.1 The penalties are as follows: _____.

(OR)

Insert the class(es).

12.2 For the _____ class(es) rules 44.1 and 44.2 are changed so that only one turn, including one tack and one gybe, is required.

Include only if the protest committee is an international jury or another provision of rule 70.4 applies. Use 'jury' only if referring to an international jury

12.3 Decisions of the [protest committee] [jury] will be final as provided in rule 70.4.

13 SCORING

Include only if the Low Point System is replaced by the Bonus Point System.

13.1 The Bonus Point System of Appendix A will apply.

(OR)

Include only if neither of the Appendix A scoring systems will be used. Describe the system.

13.1 The scoring system is as follows: _____.

Insert the number. .

13.2 _____ races are required to be completed to constitute a series.

Insert the numbers throughout.

13.3 (a) When fewer than _____ races have been completed, a boat's series score will be the total of her race scores.

(b) When from _____ to _____ races have been completed, a boat's series score will be the total of her race scores excluding her worst score.

(c) When _____ or more races have been completed, a boat's series score will be the total of her race scores excluding her two worst scores.

14 SUPPORT BOATS

Insert the identification markings. National letters are suggested for international events

Support boats shall be marked with _____.

15 BERTHING

Boats shall be kept in their assigned places in the [boat park] [harbour].

16 HAUL-OUT RESTRICTIONS

Keel boats shall not be hauled out during the regatta except with and according to the terms of prior written permission of the race committee.

17 DIVING EQUIPMENT AND PLASTIC POOLS

Underwater breathing apparatus and plastic pools or their equivalent shall not be used around keel boats between the preparatory signal of the first race and the end of the regatta.

18 RADIO COMMUNICATION

Insert any alternative text that applies. Describe the radio communication bands or frequencies that will be used or allowed.

A boat shall neither make radio transmissions while racing nor receive radio communications not available to all boats. This restriction also applies to mobile telephones.

19 PRIZES

When perpetual trophies will be awarded state their complete names.

Prizes will be given as follows: ____.

20 DISCLAIMER OF LIABILITY

Competitors participate in the regatta entirely at their own risk. See rule 4, Decision to Race. The organizing authority will not accept any liability for material damage or personal injury or death sustained in conjunction with or prior to, during, or after the regatta.

21 INSURANCE

Insert the currency and amount.

Each participating boat shall be insured with valid third-party liability insurance with a minimum cover of _____ per event or the equivalent.

22 FURTHER INFORMATION

Insert necessary contact information: person or organization, address, telephone, fax, e-mail.

For further information please contact _____.

APPENDIX L
SAILING INSTRUCTIONS GUIDE

This guide provides a set of tested sailing instructions designed primarily for major championship regattas for one or more classes. It therefore will be particularly useful for world, continental and national championships and other events of similar importance. The guide can also be useful for other events; however, for such events some of these instructions will be unnecessary or undesirable. Race officers should therefore be careful in making their choices.

An expanded version of the guide, Appendix LE, is available on the ISAF website (www.sailing.org). It contains provisions applicable to the largest and most complicated multi-class events, as well as variations on several of the sailing instructions recommended in this appendix. It will be revised from time to time, to reflect advances in race management techniques as they develop, and can be downloaded as a basic text for producing the sailing instructions for any particular event. Appendix L can also be downloaded from the ISAF website.

The principles on which all sailing instructions should be based are as follows

1. *They should include only two types of statement: the intentions of the race committee and the obligations of competitors*
2. *They should be concerned only with racing. Information about social events, assignment of moorings, etc., should be provided separately*
3. *They should not change the racing rules except when clearly desirable.*
4. *They should not repeat or restate any of the racing rules.*
5. *They should not repeat themselves.*
6. *They should be in chronological order; that is, the order in which the competitor will use them.*

7 They should, when possible, use words or phrases from the racing rules.

To use this guide, first review rule J2 and decide which instructions will be needed. Instructions that are required by rule J2.1 are marked with an asterisk (*). Delete all inapplicable or unnecessary instructions. Select the version preferred where there is a choice. Follow the directions in the left margin to fill in the spaces where a solid line (_____) appears and select the preferred wording if a choice or option is shown in brackets ([. . .]).

After deleting unused instructions, renumber all instructions in sequential order. Be sure that instruction numbers are correct where one instruction refers to another.

On separate lines, insert the full name of the regatta, the inclusive dates from measurement or the practice race until the final race or closing ceremony, the name of the organizing authority, and the city and country.

____

____

____

____

____

SAILING INSTRUCTIONS

1 RULES

1.1* The regatta will be governed by the rules as defined in *The Racing Rules of Sailing*.

Insert the name. State the relevant prescriptions in full.

1.2 The following prescriptions of the _____ national authority will apply: _____.

(OR)

Use only if the national authority for the venue of the event has not adopted a prescription to rule 87.

1.2 No national authority prescriptions will apply.

List by name any other documents that govern the event; for example, The Equipment Rules of Sailing, *to the extent that they apply.*

1.3* _____ will apply.

See rule 86. Insert the rule number(s) and state the changes.

1.4 Racing rule(s) _____ will be changed as follows: _____.

Insert the rule number(s) and class name. Make a separate statement for the rules of each class.

1.5 Rule(s) _____ of the _____ class rules [will not apply] [is (are) changed as follows: _____].

1.6 If there is a conflict between languages the English text will take precedence.

2 NOTICES TO COMPETITORS

Insert the location(s).

Notices to competitors will be posted on the official notice board(s) located at _____.

3 CHANGES TO SAILING INSTRUCTIONS

Change the times if different.

Any change to the sailing instructions will be posted before 0900 on the day it will take effect, except that any change to the schedule of races will be posted by 2000 on the day before it will take effect.

4 SIGNALS MADE ASHORE

Insert the location.

4.1 Signals made ashore will be displayed at _____.

Insert the number of minutes.

4.2 When flag AP is displayed ashore, '1 minute' is replaced with 'not less than _____ minutes' in the race signal AP.

(OR)

Insert the number of minutes.

4.2 Flag D with a sound means 'The warning signal will be made not less than ____ minutes after flag D is displayed. [Boats are requested not to leave the harbour until this signal is made.]'

Delete if a class rule applies.

4.3 When flag Y is displayed ashore, rule 40.1 applies at all times while afloat. This changes the Part 4 preamble.

5 SCHEDULE OF RACES

Revise as desired and insert the dates and classes. Include a practice race if any. When the series consists of qualifying races and final races, specify them. The schedule can also be given in an attachment.

5.1* Dates of racing:

Date	*Class ____*	*Class ____*
____	racing	racing
____	racing	reserve day
____	reserve day	racing
____	racing	racing
____	racing	racing

5.2* Number of races:

Insert the classes and numbers

Class	*Number*	*Races per day*
____	____	____
____	____	____

(a) Reserve days may be used if races are not completed as scheduled or if the race committee considers it unlikely that races will be completed as scheduled.

(b) One extra race per day may be sailed, provided that no class becomes more than one race ahead of schedule.

5.3* The scheduled time of the warning signal for

Insert the time.

the first race each day is ____.

5.4 When there has been a long postponement and when more than one race (or sequence of races, for two or more classes) will be held on the same day, the warning signal for the first race and each succeeding race will be made as soon as practicable. To alert boats that a race or sequence of races will begin soon, an orange flag will be displayed with one sound for at least four minutes before a warning signal is displayed.

5.5 On the last day of the regatta no warning signal will be made after ____.

Insert the time.

6* CLASS FLAGS

Class flags will be:

Insert the classes and names or descriptions of the flags.

Class	*Flag*
____	____
____	____
____	____

7 RACING AREAS

Attachment ____ shows the location of racing areas.

Insert a number or letter

8 THE COURSES

Insert a number or letter. A method of illustrating various courses is shown in Addendum A. Insert the course length if applicable.

8.1* The diagrams in Attachment _____ show the courses, including the approximate angles between legs, the order in which marks are to be passed, and the side on which each mark is to be left. [The approximate course length will be _____.]

8.2 No later than the warning signal, the race committee signal boat will display the approximate compass bearing of the first leg.

8.3 When there is a gate, boats shall sail between the gate marks from the direction of the previous mark and round either gate mark.

8.4 Courses will not be shortened. This changes rule 32.

Include only when changing positions of marks is impracticable.

8.5 Legs of the course will not be changed after the preparatory signal. This changes rule 33.

9 MARKS

9.1* Marks 1, 2, 3 and 4 will be _____.

Change the mark numbers as needed and insert the descriptions of the marks. Use the second alternative when Marks 4S and 4P form a gate, with Mark 4S to be left to starboard and Mark 4P to port. Unless clear from the course diagrams, state which marks are rounding marks.

(OR)

9.1* Marks 1, 2, 3, 4S and 4P will be _____.

9.2 New marks, as provided in instruction 12.1, will be _____.

Insert the descriptions of the marks.

9.3* The starting and finishing marks will be _____.

Describe the starting and finishing marks: for example, the race committee signal boat at the starboard end and a buoy at the port end. Instruction 11.2 will describe the starting line and instruction 13 the finishing line.

9.4 A race committee boat signalling a change of a leg of the course is a mark as provided in instruction 12.2.

10 AREAS THAT ARE OBSTRUCTIONS

The following areas are designated as obstructions: _____.

Describe each area by its location and any easily recognized details of appearance.

11 THE START

11.1 Races will be started by using rule 26 with the warning signal given _____ minutes before the starting signal.

Include only if the asterisked option in rule 26 will be used. Insert the number of minutes..

(OR)

11.1 Races will be started by using rule 26 with the following addition:
An attention signal (flag F with one sound) will be made five minutes before the warning signal for the first class to start. The race committee will designate the course to be sailed before or with the attention signal. Flag F will be removed with one sound one minute before the warning signal. This changes rule 27.1.

For large fleets and long starting lines.

(OR)

11.1 Races will be started as follows: _____. This changes rule 26.

Describe any starting system other than that stated in rule 26.

11.2* The starting line will be between staffs displaying orange flags on the starting marks..

(OR)

11.2* The starting line will be between a staff displaying an orange flag on the starting mark at the starboard-end and the port-end starting mark.

(OR)

11.2* The starting line will be _____.

Insert the description.

11.3 Boats whose warning signal has not been made shall avoid the starting area.

11.4 A boat starting later than _____ minutes after her starting signal will be scored Did Not Start. This changes rule A4.

Insert the number of minutes.

11.5 If any part of a boat's hull, crew or equipment is on the course side of the starting line during the two minutes before her starting signal, the race committee will display flag V. It will be displayed until all boats have sailed completely to the pre-start side, but not after the starting signal.

(OR)

11.5 If any part of a boat's hull, crew or equipment is on the course side of the starting line during the two minutes before her starting signal and she is identified, the race committee will attempt to broadcast her sail number on VHF channel - _____. Failure to make a broadcast or to time it accurately will not be grounds for a request for redress. This changes rule 62.1(a).

Insert the channel number.

12 CHANGE OF THE NEXT LEG OF THE COURSE

12.1 To change the next leg of the course, the race committee will move the original mark (or the finishing line) to a new position.

(OR)

12.1 To change the next leg of the course, the race

committee will lay a new mark (or move the finishing line) and remove the original mark as soon as practicable. When in a subsequent change a new mark is replaced, it will be replaced by an original mark.

Reverse 'port' and 'starboard' when the mark is to be left to starboard.

12.2 Except at a gate, boats shall pass between the race committee boat signalling the change of the next leg and the nearby mark, leaving the mark to port and the race committee boat to starboard. This changes rule 28.1.

13* THE FINISH

The finishing line will be between staffs displaying orange flags on the finishing marks.

(OR)

The finishing line will be between a staff displaying an orange flag on the finishing mark at the starboard-end and the port-end finishing mark.

(OR)

Insert the description

The finishing line will be _____.

14 PENALTY SYSTEM

Include instruction 14.1 only when the Two-Turns Penalty will not be used. Insert the number of places or describe the penalties.

14.1 The Scoring Penalty, rule 44.3, will apply. The penalty will be _____ places.

(OR)

14.1 The penalties are as follows: _____.

Insert the class(es).

14.2 For the _____ class(es) rules 44.1 and 44.2 are changed so that only one turn, including one tack and one gybe, is required.

14.3 A boat that has taken a penalty under rule 31.2 or 44.1 shall complete an acknowledgment form at the race office within the protest time limit.

Here and below, use 'jury' only when referring to an international jury.

14.4 As provided in rule 67, the [protest committee] [jury] may, without a hearing, penalize a boat that has broken rule 42.

(OR)

14.4 Appendix P will apply [as changed by instruction(s)] [14.2] [and] [14.5].

Recommended only for junior events

14.5 Rule P2.3 will not apply and rule P2.2 is changed so that it will apply to any protest after the first one.

15 TIME LIMITS

15.1* Time limits are as follows:

Insert the classes and times. Omit the Mark 1 time limit if inapplicable.

Class	*Time limit*	*Mark 1 time limit*
_____	_____	_____
_____	_____	_____
_____	_____	_____

If no boat has passed Mark 1 within the Mark 1 time limit the race will be abandoned.

Insert the time (or different times for different classes).

15.2 Boats failing to finish within _____ after the first boat sails the course and finishes will be scored Did Not Finish. This changes rules 35 and A4.

16 PROTESTS AND REQUESTS FOR REDRESS

16.1 Protest forms are available at the race office. Protests shall be delivered there within the protest time limit.

Change the time if different.

16.2 For each class, the protest time limit is 90 minutes after the last boat has finished the last race of the day. [The same time limit applies to protests by the race committee and [protest committee] [jury] about incidents they observe in the racing area and to requests for redress. This changes rules 61.3 and 62.2.]

Change the posting time if different. Insert the jury room location and the time for the first hearing.

16.3 Notices will be posted within 30 minutes of the protest time limit to inform competitors of hearings in which they are parties or named as witnesses. Hearings will be held in the jury room, located at _____, beginning at _____.

16.4 Notices of protests by the race committee or [protest committee] [jury] will be posted to inform boats under rule 61.1(b).

16.5 A list of boats that, under instruction 14.4, have acknowledged breaking rule 42 or have been disqualified by the [protest committee] [jury] will be posted before the protest time limit.

16.6 Breaches of instructions 11.3, 14.3, 18, 19.2, 22, 23 and 24 will not be grounds for a protest by a boat. This changes rule 60.1(a). Penalties for these breaches may be less than disqualification if the [protest committee] [jury] so decides.

16.7 On the last day of the regatta a request for reopening a hearing shall be delivered

(a) within the protest time limit if the party requesting reopening was informed of the decision on the previous day;

(b) no later than 30 minutes after the party requesting reopening was informed of the decision on that day.

Change the time if different.

This changes rule 66.

16.8 Decisions of the [protest committee] [jury] will be final as provided in rule 70.4.

Include only if the protest committee is an international jury or another provision of rule 70.4 applies.

17 SCORING

17.1* The Bonus Point System of Appendix A will apply.

Include only if the Low Point System is replaced by the Bonus Point System.

(OR)

17.1* The scoring system is as follows: _____.

Include only if neither of the Appendix A scoring systems will be used. Describe the system.

17.2* _____ races are required to be completed to constitute a series.

Insert the number.

17.3 (a) When fewer than _____ races have been completed, a boat's series score will be the total of her race scores.

Insert the numbers throughout.

(b) When from _____ to _____ races have been completed, a boat's series score will be the total of her race scores excluding her worst score.

(c) When _____ or more races have been completed, a boat's series score will be the total of her race scores excluding her two worst scores.

18 SAFETY REGULATIONS

18.1 Check-out and check-in: _____.

Insert the procedure for check-out and check-in.

18.2 A boat that retires from a race shall notify the race committee as soon as possible.

19 REPLACEMENT OF CREW OR EQUIPMENT

19.1 Substitution of competitors will not be allowed without prior written approval of the [race committee] [protest committee] [jury].

19.2 Substitution of damaged or lost equipment will not be allowed unless approved by the race committee. Requests for substitution shall be made to the committee at the first reasonable opportunity.

20 EQUIPMENT AND MEASUREMENT CHECKS

A boat or equipment may be inspected at any time for compliance with the class rules and sailing instructions. On the water, a boat can be instructed by a race committee measurer to proceed immediately to a designated area for inspection.

21 OFFICIAL BOATS

Official boats will be marked as follows: _____.

Insert the descriptions. If appropriate, use different identification markings for boats performing different duties.

22 SUPPORT BOATS

22.1 Team leaders, coaches and other support

personnel shall stay outside areas where boats are racing from the time of the preparatory signal for the first class to start until all boats have finished or the race committee signals a postponement, general recall or abandonment.

22.2 Support boats shall be marked with _____.

Insert the identification markings. National letters are suggested for international events.

23 HAUL-OUT RESTRICTIONS

Keel boats shall not be hauled out during the regatta except with and according to the terms of prior written permission of the race committee.

24 DIVING EQUIPMENT AND PLASTIC POOLS

Underwater breathing apparatus and plastic pools or their equivalent shall not be used around keel boats between the preparatory signal of the first race and the end of the regatta.

25 RADIO COMMUNICATION

A boat shall neither make radio transmissions while racing nor receive radio communications not available to all boats. This restriction also applies to mobile telephones.

Insert any alternative text that applies. Describe the radio communication bands or frequencies that will be used or allowed.

26 PRIZES

Prizes will be given as follows: _____.

If perpetual trophies will be awarded state their complete names.

27 DISCLAIMER OF LIABILITY

Competitors participate in the regatta entirely at their own risk. See rule 4, Decision to Race. The organizing authority will not accept any liability for material damage or personal injury or death sustained in conjunction with or prior to, during, or after the regatta.

28 INSURANCE

Insert the currency and amount.

Each participating boat shall be insured with valid third-party liability insurance with a minimum cover of _____ per event or the equivalent.

Addendum A - Illustrating the Course

Shown here are diagrams of course shapes. Any course can be similarly shown. When there is more than one course, prepare a separate diagram for each course and state how each will be signalled.

A Windward-Leeward Course

Start - 1 - 2 - 1 - 2 - Finish

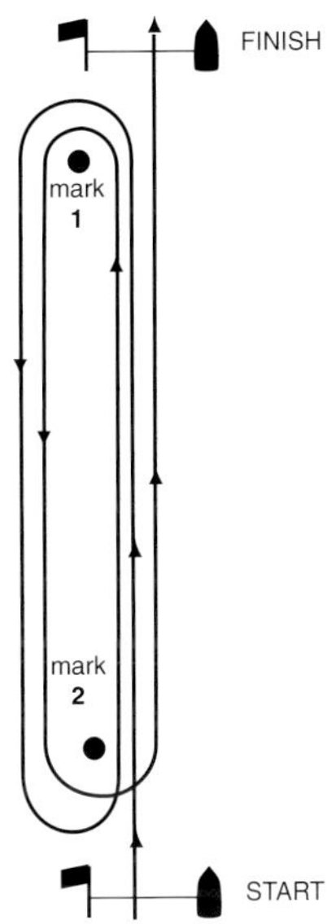

Options for this course include

(1) *increasing or decreasing the number of laps,*

(2) *deleting the final windward leg,*

(3) *using a gate instead of a leeward mark*

(4) *using an offset mark at the windward mark, and*

(5) *using the leeward and windward marks as starting and finishing marks*

A Windward-Leeward-Triangle Course

Start - 1 - 2 - 3 - 1 - 3 - Finish

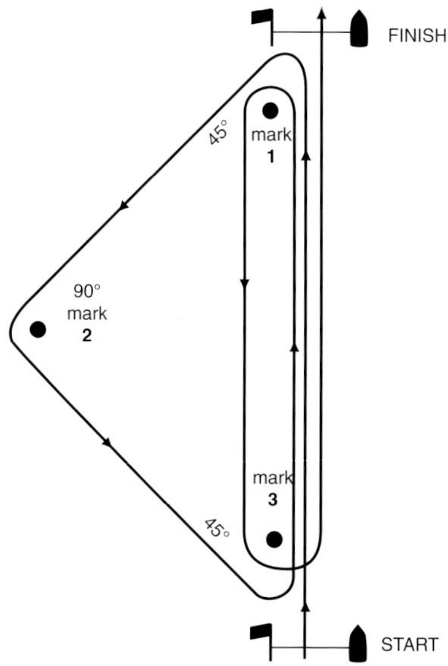

Options for this course include

(1) increasing or decreasing the number of laps

(2) deleting the last windward leg

(3) varying the interior angles of the triangle (45°–90°–45° and 60°–60°–60° are common),

(4) using a gate instead of a leeward mark for downwind legs (but not reaches),

(5) using an offset mark at the beginning of downwind legs (but not reaches), and

(6) using the leeward and windward marks as starting and finishing marks

Be sure to specify the interior angle at each mark.

Trapezoid Courses

Start - 1 - 2 - 3 - 2 - 3 - Finish Start - 1 - 4 - 1 - 2 - 3 - Finish

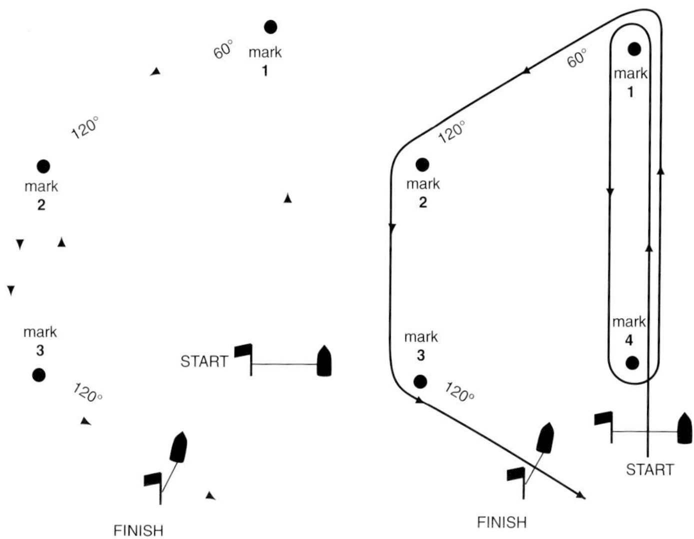

Options for these courses include

(1) adding additional legs

(2) using gates instead of leeward marks for downwind legs (but not reaches),

(3) varying the interior angles of the reaching legs,

(4) using an offset mark at the beginning of downwind legs (but not reaches), and

(5) finishing boats upwind rather than on a reach

Be sure to specify the interior angle of each reaching leg. It is recommended that Mark 4 be different from the starting mark

Addendum B - Boats Provided by the Organizing Authority

The following sailing instruction is recommended when all boats will be provided by the organizing authority. It can be changed to suit the circumstances. When used, it should be inserted after instruction 3.

4 BOATS

4.1 Boats will be provided for all competitors, who shall not modify them or cause them to be modified in any way except that

(a) a compass may be tied or taped to the hull or spars;

(b) wind indicators, including yarn or thread, may be tied or taped anywhere on the boat;

(c) hulls, centreboards and rudders may be cleaned, but only with water;

(d) adhesive tape may be used anywhere above the water line; and

(e) all fittings or equipment designed to be adjusted may be adjusted, provided that the class rules are complied with.

4.2 All equipment provided with the boat for sailing purposes shall be in the boat while afloat.

4.3 The penalty for not complying with one of the above instructions will be disqualification from all races sailed in which the instruction was broken.

4.4 Competitors shall report any damage or loss of equipment, however slight, to the organizing authority's representative immediately after securing the boat ashore. The penalty for breaking this instruction, unless the [protest committee] [jury] is satisfied that the competitor made a determined effort to comply, will be disqualification from the race most recently sailed.

4.5 Class rules requiring competitors to be members of the class association will not apply.

Addendum C (RYA) - Gate Start

The following sailing instruction is recommended when a gate start is required.

1 When flag G is displayed on the race committee boat a gate start will be used.

2 A starting mark will be laid at the leeward end of the gate.

3 The gate launch will display flag G and the guard launch will display flag U. Starting signals will be made on the race committee boat.

4 The pathfinder for the first race will be nominated by the race committee.

Subsequently, the pathfinder will be the tenth boat in the preceding race. When she is unable to race, or has been the pathfinder previously in the event, the pathfinder will be the eleventh boat in the preceding race and so on. Her number will be posted on the official notice board. The pathfinder shall report to the gate launch five minutes before the warning signal.

5 At or around the starting signal the pathfinder will sail from the starting mark on a close-hauled port tack. During the start the pathfinder will be followed by the gate launch and the guard launch will keep station off the pathfinder's starboard bow.

6 The starting line will be between the starting mark and the stern of the gate launch.

7 The pathfinder shall maintain her course until released by the race officer.

Insert the time

8 After the release of the pathfinder, the gate launch will maintain her course and speed until _____ minutes after the starting signal, When she stops she will lower flag G half way and make a sound signal.

9 A boat not having correctly started which is on the port side of the gate launch while the gate is opening, shall not cross the starting line from the course side.

10 After the preparatory signal a boat which interferes with or tries to pass between the pathfinder and the gate or guard launch, or that causes another boat to interfere in these ways, will be disqualified without a hearing. If the race is restarted, resailed or rescheduled she is not entitled to compete. This changes Rule 63.1.

11 The gate launch, the guard launch and the pathfinder until release, rank as starting marks.

12 A boat that cannot avoid touching a starting mark may hail a right-of-way boat for room and shall retire.

Insert the time

13 A boat shall not start later than _____ minutes after the starting signal when flag G on the gate launch and the race committee boat will be lowered.

Addendum D (RYA) Time Penalty

The RYA recommends the use of the Time Penalty when it is not practicable to use the Turns Penalty, when the automatic loss of places is thought to make the Scoring Penalty too severe and when the elapsed times of boats are recorded. A time penalty may also be used for touching a mark when it is not practicable for a boat to perform a turn. The sailing instruction may be varied to specify a different percentage, or that the percentage be added to her corrected time, or that a stated number of seconds be added to her elapsed or corrected time.

Time Penalty

Rule 44, [and rule 31.2] will not apply. A boat that may have broken a rule of Part 2 while *racing* [or that has broken rule 31.1] may take a Time Penalty, unless she has caused injury or serious damage or gained a significant advantage in the race or series in which case she shall retire. The Time Penalty will be to add 1% of her elapsed time to her elapsed time, rounding the increased time to the nearest second.

Rules 44.3(a) and (b) apply, substituting Time Penalty for Scoring Penalty throughout.

Rule 44.4 is amended to read:

(a) When a boat intends to take a Time Penalty for breaking a rule of Part 2 and in the same incident has touched a *mark* she need not take the penalty for breaking rule 31.1.

(b) A boat that takes a penalty shall not be penalized further with respect to the same incident unless she failed to retire when this sailing instruction required her to do so.

(c) A boat shall not be scored as having *finished* outside a time limit solely by the application of a time penalty.

APPENDIX M
RECOMMENDATIONS FOR PROTEST COMMITTEES

This appendix is advisory only; in some circumstances changing these procedures may be advisable. It is addressed primarily to protest committee chairmen but may also help judges, jury secretaries, race committees and others connected with protest and redress hearings.

In a protest or redress hearing, the protest committee should weigh all testimony with equal care; should recognize that honest testimony can vary, and even be in conflict, as a result of different observations and recollections; should resolve such differences as best it can; should recognize that no boat or competitor is guilty until a breach of a *rule* has been established to the satisfaction of the protest committee; and should keep an open mind until all the evidence has been heard as to whether a boat or competitor has broken a *rule*.

M1 PRELIMINARIES (may be performed by race office staff)

- Receive the *protest* or request for redress.
- Note on the form the time the *protest* or request is delivered and the protest time limit.
- Inform each *party*, and the race committee when necessary, when and where the hearing will be held.

M2 BEFORE THE HEARING

Make sure that

- each *party* has a copy of or the opportunity to read the *protest* or request for redress and has had reasonable time to prepare for the hearing.

- no member of the protest committee is an *interested party*. Ask the *parties* whether they object to any member. When redress is requested under rule 62.1(a), a member of the race committee should not be a member of the protest committee.
- only one person from each boat (or *party*) is present unless an interpreter is needed.
- all boats and people involved are present. If they are not, however, the committee may proceed under rule 63.3(b).
- boats' representatives were on board when required (rule 63.3(a)). When the *parties* were in different races, both organizing authorities must accept the composition of the protest committee (rule 63.8). In a measurement protest obtain the current class rules and identify the authority responsible for interpreting them (rule 64.3(b)).

M3 THE HEARING

M3.1 Check the validity of the *protest* or request for redress.

- Are the contents adequate (rule 61.2 or 62.1)?
- Was it delivered in time? If not, is there good reason to extend the time limit (rule 61.3 or 62.2)?
- When required, was the protestor involved in or a witness to the incident (rule 60.1(a))?
- When necessary, was 'Protest' hailed and, if required, a red flag displayed correctly (rule 61.1(a))?
- When the flag and hail were not necessary was the protestee informed?
- Decide whether the *protest* or request for redress is valid (rule 63.5).
- Once the validity of the *protest* or request has been determined, do not let the subject be introduced again unless truly new evidence is available.

M3.2 Take the evidence (rule 63.6).

- Ask the protestor and then the protestee to tell their stories. Then allow them to question one another. In a redress matter, ask the *party* to state the request.
- Invite questions from protest committee members.
- Make sure you know what facts each *party* is alleging before calling any witnesses. Their stories may be different.
- Allow anyone, including a boat's crew, to give evidence. It is the *party* who normally decides which witnesses to call, although the protest committee may also call witnesses (rule 63.6). The question asked by a *party* 'Would you like to hear N?' is best answered by 'It is your choice.'
- Call each *party's* witnesses (and the protest committee's if any) one by one. Limit *parties* to questioning the witness(es) (they may wander into general statements).
- Invite the protestee to question the protestor's witness first (and vice versa). This prevents the protestor from leading his witness from the beginning.
- Allow a member of the protest committee who saw the incident to give evidence (rule 63.6) but only in the presence of the *parties*. The member may be questioned and may remain in the room (rule 63.3(a)).
- Try to prevent leading questions or hearsay evidence, but if that is impossible discount the evidence so obtained.
- Accept written evidence from a witness who is not available to be questioned only if all *parties* agree. In doing so they forego their rights to question that witness (rule 63.6).
- Ask one member of the committee to note down evidence, particularly times, distances, speeds, etc.
- Invite first the protestor and then the protestee to make a final statement of her case, particularly on any application or interpretation of the *rules*.

M3.3 Find the facts (rule 63.6).

- Write down the facts; resolve doubts one way or the other.
- Call back *parties* for more questions if necessary.
- When appropriate, draw a diagram of the incident using the facts you have found.

M3.4 Decide the *protest* or request for redress (rule 64).

- Base the decision on the facts found (if you cannot, find some more facts).
- In redress cases, make sure that no further evidence is needed from boats that will be affected by the decision.

M3.5 Inform the *parties* (rule 65).

- Recall the *parties* and read them the facts found, conclusions and *rules* that apply, and the decision. When time presses it is permissible to read the decision and give the details later.
- Give any party a copy of the decision on request. File the protest or request for redress with the committee records.

M4 REOPENING A HEARING (rule 66)

When a *party*, within the time limit, has asked for a hearing to be reopened, hear the *party* making the request, look at any video, etc., and decide whether there is any material new evidence that might lead you to change your decision. Decide whether your interpretation of the *rules* may have been wrong; be open-minded as to whether you have made a mistake. If none of these applies refuse to reopen; otherwise schedule a hearing.

M5 GROSS MISCONDUCT (rule 69)

M5.1 An action under this rule is not a *protest*, but the protest committee gives its allegations in writing to the competitor before the hearing. The hearing is conducted under the same rules as other hearings but the protest committee must have at least three members (rule 69.1(b)). Use the greatest care to protect the competitor's rights.

M5.2 A competitor or a boat cannot protest under rule 69, but the protest form of a competitor who tries to do so may be accepted as a report to the protest committee, which can then decide whether or not to call a hearing.

M5.3 When it is desirable to call a hearing under rule 69 as a result of a Part 2 incident, it is important to hear any boat-vs.-boat *protest* in the normal way, deciding which boat, if any, broke which *rule*, before proceeding against the competitor under this rule.

M5.4 Although action under rule 69 is taken against a competitor, not a boat, a boat may also be penalized (rule 69.1(b)).

M5.5 The protest committee may warn the competitor (rule 69.1(b)), in which case no report is to be made to national authorities (rule 69.1(c)). When a penalty is imposed and a report is made to national authorities, it may be helpful to recommend whether or not further action should be taken.

M6 APPEALS (rule 70 and Appendix F)

When decisions can be appealed,

- retain the papers relevant to the hearing so that the information can easily be used for an appeal. Is there a diagram endorsed or prepared by the protest committee? Are the facts found sufficient? (Example: Was there an *overlap*? Yes or No. 'Perhaps' is not a fact found.) Are the names of the protest committee members and other important information on the form?
- comments by the protest committee on any appeal should enable the appeals committee to picture the whole incident clearly; the appeals committee knows nothing about the situation.

M7 PHOTOGRAPHIC EVIDENCE

Photographs and videotapes can sometimes provide useful evidence but protest committees should recognize their limitations and note the following points:

- The *party* producing the photographic evidence is responsible for arranging the viewing.
- View the tape several times to extract all the information from it.
- The depth perception of any single-lens camera is very poor; with a telephoto lens it is non-existent. When the camera views two *overlapped* boats at right angles to their course, it is impossible to assess the distance between them. When the camera views them head on, it is impossible to see whether an *overlap* exists unless it is substantial.
- Ask the following questions:
  - Where was the camera in relation to the boats?
  - Was the camera's platform moving? If so in what direction and how fast?
  - Is the angle changing as the boats approach the critical point? Fast panning causes radical change.
  - Did the camera have an unrestricted view throughout?

APPENDIX N
INTERNATIONAL JURIES

See rules 70.4 and 90(b). This appendix shall not be changed by sailing instructions or prescriptions of national authorities.

N1 COMPOSITION, APPOINTMENT AND ORGANIZATION

N1.1 An international jury shall be composed of experienced sailors with excellent knowledge of the racing rules and extensive protest committee experience. It shall be independent of and have no members from the race committee, and be appointed by the organizing authority, subject to approval by the national authority if required (see rule 90(b)), or by the ISAF under rule 88.2(b).

N1.2 The jury shall consist of a chairman, a vice chairman if desired, and other members for a total of at least five. A majority shall be International Judges. The jury may appoint a secretary, who shall not be a member of the jury.

N1.3 No more than two members (three, in Groups M, N and Q) shall be from the same national authority.

N1.4 (a) A jury of ten or more members may divide itself into two or more panels of at least five members each, of which the majority shall be International Judges. If this is done, the requirements for membership of a full jury shall apply to each panel but not to the jury as a whole.

(b) A jury of fewer than ten members may divide itself into two or three panels of at least three members each, of which the majority shall be International Judges. Members of each panel shall be from at least three different national authorities except in Groups M, N and Q, where they shall be from at least two different national authorities. If dissatisfied with a panel's decision, a *party* is entitled to a hearing by a jury composed in compliance with rules N1.1, N1.2 and N1.3, except concerning the facts found, if requested within the time limit specified in the sailing instructions.

N1.5 When a full jury has fewer than five members, because of illness or emergency, and no qualified replacements are available, it remains properly constituted if it consists of at least three members. At least two members shall be International Judges. When there are three or four members they shall be from at least three different national authorities except in Groups M, N and Q, where they shall be from at least two different national authorities.

N1.6 When the national authority's approval is required for the appointment of an international jury (see rule 90(b)), notice of its approval shall be included in the sailing instructions or be posted on the official notice board.

N1.7 If the jury acts while not properly constituted, the jury's decisions may be appealed.

N2 RESPONSIBILITIES

N2.1 An international jury is responsible for hearing and deciding all *protests*, requests for redress and other matters arising under the rules of Part 5. When asked by the organizing authority or the race committee, it shall advise and assist them on any matter directly affecting the fairness of the competition.

N2.2 Unless the organizing authority directs otherwise, the jury shall

(a) decide questions of eligibility, measurement or boat certificates; and

(b) authorize the substitution of competitors, boats, sails or equipment.

N2.3 If so directed by the organizing authority, the jury shall

(a) make or approve changes to the sailing instructions,

(b) supervise or direct the race committee in the conduct of the races, and

(c) decide on other matters referred to it by the organizing authority.

N3 PROCEDURES

N3.1 Decisions of the jury shall be made by a simple majority vote of all members. When there is an equal division of votes cast, the chairman of the meeting may cast an additional vote.

N3.2 When it is considered desirable that some members not participate in discussing and deciding a *protest* or request for redress, and no qualified replacements are available, the jury remains properly constituted if at least three members remain. At least two members shall be International Judges.

N3.3 Members shall not be regarded as *interested parties* (see rule 63.4) by reason of their nationality.

N3.4 If a panel fails to agree on a decision it may adjourn and refer the matter to the full jury.

APPENDIX P
IMMEDIATE PENALTIES FOR BREAKING RULE 42

This appendix applies only if the sailing instructions so state.

P1 PROTESTS

A member of the protest committee or its designated observer who sees a boat breaking rule 42 may protest her by, as soon as reasonably possible, making a sound signal, pointing a yellow flag at her and hailing her sail number, even if she is no longer *racing*. A boat so protested is not subject to another *protest* under rule 42 for the same incident.

P2 PENALTIES

P2.1 First Protest

When a boat is first protested under rule P1 she may acknowledge her breach by taking a Two-Turns Penalty under rule 44.2. If she fails to do so she shall be disqualified without a hearing.

P2.2 Second Protest

When a boat is protested a second time during the series she may acknowledge her breach by immediately retiring from the race. If she fails to do so she shall be disqualified without a hearing and her score shall not be excluded.

P2.3 Third Protest

When a boat is protested a third time during the series she may acknowledge her breach by immediately retiring from the race and from all other races in the series. If she fails to do so she shall be disqualified without a hearing from all races in the series, with no score excluded, and the protest committee shall consider calling a hearing under rule 69.1(a).

P3 POSTPONEMENT, GENERAL RECALL OR ABANDONMENT

If a boat has been protested under rule P1 and the race committee signals a *postponement*, general recall or *abandonment*, the penalty from her first or second *protest* is cancelled, but the *protest* is counted to determine the number of times she has been protested during the series..

ISAF REGULATIONS

The ISAF Regulations printed in this section are also racing rules. They are correct at August 2004 but may be amended at any meeting of the ISAF Council. Any amendment will be announced on the RYA website (www.rya.org.uk/racing/rules.asp) and posted on the ISAF website (www.sailing.org). The RYA Prescriptions may also change as a consequence.

REGULATION 19 ELIGIBILITY CODE

See rule 75.2.

19 ELIGIBILITY CODE

ISAF ELIGIBILITY RULES

19.1 A competitor whose ISAF eligibility has been suspended or revoked shall not engage in any competition in the sport of sailing.

19.2 To be eligible to compete in an event listed in 19.3, a competitor shall:

(a) be governed by the regulations and rules of ISAF;

(b) be a member of his/her Member National Authority or one of its affiliated organizations. Such membership shall be established by the competitor;

(i) being entered by a national authority of the country of which the competitor is a national or ordinarily a resident; or

(ii) presenting a valid membership card or certificate, or other satisfactory evidence of identity and membership.

(c) (i) be registered as an 'ISAF Sailor' on the ISAF Website; and

(ii) sign the waiver from the Court for Arbitration in Sport

For those events listed under 19.3(a), (b) and (c), Olympic Qualification Events and ISAF Graded Match Racing Events.

EVENTS REQUIRING ISAF ELIGIBILITY

19.3. ISAF Eligibility is required for the following events:

(a) the sailing regatta of the Olympic Games;

(b) the sailing regattas of Regional Games recognized by the International Olympic Committee;

(c) events including ISAF in their titles;

(d) world and continental championships of ISAF classes and world championships of the IMS, Major Events and other events approved by ISAF as a World Championship;

(e) any event at which the Organizing Authority, Member National Authority or ISAF has appointed an International Jury or International Umpires, International Race Officers, International Measurers or ISAF Technical Delegates to serve in their capacity for which they hold a Certificate of Appointment issued by ISAF;

(f) any event approved by a Member National Authority of the ISAF as an Olympic qualifying event; and

(g) any event designated by a Member National Authority within its jurisdiction as requiring ISAF eligibility.

19.3.1 With the approval of the relevant Member National Authority, an Organizing Authority may also require ISAF eligibility for an event when so stated in the notice of race and sailing instructions.

SUSPENSION OF ISAF ELIGIBILITY

19.4 After proper inquiry by either the national authority of the competitor or the ISAF Executive Committee, a competitor's ISAF eligibility shall be promptly suspended with immediate effect, permanently or for a specified period of time

(a) for any suspension of eligibility in accordance with RRS 69.2; or

(b) for breaking RRS 5; or

(c) for competing, within the two years preceding the inquiry, in an event that the competitor knew or should have known was a prohibited event.

19.4.1 A prohibited event is an event:

(a) permitting or requiring advertising beyond that permitted by the ISAF Advertising Code;

(b) with prizes or other benefits referred to in Regulation 18.16.1 that is a national event not approved by the national authority of the venue or an international event not approved by the ISAF;

(c) that is described as a world championship or uses the word 'world', either in the title of the event or otherwise, and that is not approved by the ISAF; or

(d) that does not conform to the requirements of RRS 87, and is not otherwise approved by the ISAF.

19.4.2 When an event described in regulation 19.3 has been approved as required, that fact shall be stated in the notice of race and the sailing instructions.

REPORTS; REVIEWS; NOTIFICATION; APPEALS

19.5 When a national authority suspends a competitor's ISAF eligibility under regulation 19.4, it shall promptly report the suspension and reasons therefor to the ISAF. The ISAF Executive Committee may revise or annul the suspension with immediate effect. The ISAF shall promptly report any suspension of a competitor's eligibility, or of its revision or annulment by the ISAF Executive Committee, to all National Authorities, ISAF Class Associations and other ISAF affiliated organizations, which may also suspend eligibility for events held within their jurisdiction.

19.5.1 A competitor whose suspension of ISAF eligibility has been either imposed by a national authority, or imposed or revised by the ISAF Executive Committee, shall be advised of the right to appeal to the ISAF Review Board and be provided with a copy of the Review Board Rules of Procedure.

19.5.2 A national authority or the ISAF Executive Committee may ask for a review of its decision by the ISAF Review Board by complying with the Review Board Rules of Procedure.

19.5.3 The Review Board Rules of Procedure shall govern all appeals and requests for review.

19.5.4 Upon an appeal or request for review, the ISAF Review Board may confirm, revise or annul a suspension of eligibility, or require a hearing or rehearing by the suspending authority.

19.5.5 Decisions of the Review Board may be appealed in accordance with Article 84. (Note Article 84 to be amended in November 2004).

19.5.6 The ISAF shall promptly notify all national authorities, ISAF Class Associations and other ISAF affiliated organizations of all Review Board decisions.

REINSTATEMENT OF ISAF ELIGIBILITY

19.6 The ISAF Review Board may reinstate the ISAF eligibility of a competitor who:

(a) applies for reinstatement;

(b) establishes substantial, changed circumstances justifying reinstatement; and

(c) has completed a minimum of three years of suspension.

CLASS ELIGIBILITY

19.7 Any competitor whose eligibility has been suspended, denied, or revoked by an ISAF Class may appeal that decision to the ISAF Review Board in accordance with Articles 81, 83 and 84 and ISAF Regulation 19.5.

REGULATION 20
ADVERTISING CODE

See rule 79.

20 ADVERTISING CODE

DEFINITION OF ADVERTISING

20.1 For the purposes of this code, advertising is the name, logo, slogan, description, depiction, a variation or distortion thereof, or any other form of communication that promotes an organization, person, product, service, brand or idea so as to call attention to it or to persuade persons or organizations to buy, approve or otherwise support it.

GENERAL

20.2 Advertising shall not be displayed on a boat, except as required or permitted by the ISAF Advertising Code.

20.2.1 Advertisements and anything advertised shall meet generally accepted moral and ethical standards.

20.2.2 Advertisements on sails shall be clearly separated from national letters and sail numbers.

20.2.3 The ISAF Advertising Code does not apply at the Olympic Regatta, at which the International Olympic Committee charter applies.

ADVERTISING

20.3 The following types of advertising are permitted or required as stated and apply at all times:

(a) Boats and Sailboards

The class insignia shall be displayed on her sails as required by RRS Appendix G;

(b) (i) Boats

One sailmaker's mark, which may include the name or mark of the sailcloth manufacturer and the pattern or model of the sail, may be displayed on both sides of any sail and shall fit within a 150mm x 150mm square. On sails, other than spinnakers, no part of such mark shall be placed farther from the tack point than the greater of 300mm or 15% of the length of the foot;

(ii) Sailboards

One sailmaker's mark, which may include the name or mark of the sailcloth manufacturer and the pattern or model of the sail, may be displayed on both sides of the sail and shall fit within a 150mm x 150mm square. No part of such mark shall be placed farther from the tack point than 20% of the length of the foot of the sail, including the mast sleeve. The mark may also be displayed on the lower half of the part of the sail above the wishbone (boom) but no part of it shall be farther than 500mm from the clew point;

(c) (i) Boats

One builder's mark, which may include the name or mark of the designer, may be placed on each side of the hull, and one maker's mark may be displayed on each side on spars and on each side of other equipment. Such marks shall fit within a 150mm x 150mm square;

(ii) Sailboards

Any number of manufacturers' names or logos may be placed on the board (hull) and in two places on the upper third of the part of the sail above the wishbone (boom). One maker's mark may be displayed each side on spars, and on each side of any other equipment;

(d) (i) Boats

The forward part of the hull on each side of all participating boats in an event shall only display advertising chosen and required to be displayed by that event organizer as follows:

- for boats under 6.5 metres, 25% of the *hull length*, and
- for boats over 6.5 metres, 20% of the *hull length*

excluding *bow numbers*. If such advertising is required, it shall be so stated in the Notice of Race. If advertising is for alcohol or tobacco, the word 'may' instead of 'shall' applies;

(ii) Sailboards

There shall be no reserved hull space on sailboards for event organizers.

The *organizing authority* of a sponsored event may permit or require the display of an advertisement of the event on both sides of the sail between the sail numbers and the wishbone (boom), on both sides of the sail aft of the foot median and on a bib worn by the competitors;

(e) competitors may display advertising on clothing and personal equipment without restriction.

20.3.1 In addition to 20.3, additional advertising chosen by the individual boat may be displayed in the following categories:

(a) Category A

No additional advertising.

(b) Category C

Advertising is permitted as per Category A, and in addition on hulls, spars and sails without restriction except the space reserved for identification by Appendix G and under section 20.3(b), (c) and (d).

20.3.2 When equipment is supplied by the event's *organizing authority*, Category C advertising on the supplied equipment is available to the *organizing authority*. Where a bib, or its equivalent, is supplied at an event, it may be worn at the absolute discretion of the individual competitor.

ALL CLASSES (EXCEPT WHEN PARTICIPATING IN EVENTS LISTED IN REGULATION 20.6.1) - ISAF AND NON-ISAF STATUS, NATIONAL CLASSES

20.4 The right to choose Category A or C applies to all ISAF *Classes*, except Olympic Classes which shall be unrestricted Category C.

20.4.1 (a) The Class Associations of ISAF *Classes* may decide the advertising category to be applied to their class to be either A or C. If the Class Association makes no ruling, Category A shall apply;

(b) The Class Associations of Non-ISAF *Classes* (excluding *National Classes* referred to in Regulation 20.4.1(c) below) may decide the advertising category to be applied to their Class to be either A or C. If the Class Association makes no ruling, Category A shall apply;

(c) For *National Classes* the National Authority of the *Class* decides Category A or C. If the National Authority makes no ruling, Category A shall apply.

20.4.2 If Category C status is chosen, only the National Authority may introduce an Individual Advertising License System to permit its *competitors* to display advertising on their boats/sailboards. (A breach of a National Authority's license system is not protestable under this Code).

20.4.3 For *club or invitational events* the *organizing authority* may restrict advertising to Category A, with the approval of the National Authority of the organizing club. Where the event includes a class that has been chosen as equipment for the forthcoming Olympic Regatta, the limitations of Regulation 20.4.3 do not apply to that specific Olympic class, unless approved by the ISAF Executive Committee.

20.4.4 If Category C is decided, the ISAF Classes (except for Olympic Classes) and non-ISAF Classes (*including National Classes*) may decide the maximum level of advertising. Any restrictions within Category C shall be included in the Class Rules and subject to a recommendation by the ISAF Executive Committee and ISAF Council's approval. Olympic Classes cannot restrict Category C in any way.

20.4.5 Except as provided by Regulations 20.3 and 20.3.2 the right to have any or all advertising on the hulls, sails and spars shall be solely the right of and at the direction of the *competitor* provided that such right may be contracted or assigned to others at the competitor's discretion.

HANDICAPPING SYSTEMS AND RATING RULES

20.5 The National Authority of a *competitor* in respect of the boat in which the *competitor* is competing, may decide the advertising category to be applied to boats racing under a handicap/measurement system to be either A or C. If Category C is decided, the said *competitor's* National Authority may decide the maximum level of advertising. If the National Authority makes no ruling, Category A shall apply.

Any *Class* (see definition of Class) or individual boat racing under a handicap/measurement system shall have its advertising category determined in accordance with the provisions of this clause.

20.5.1 For the purposes of Regulation 20.5, the provisions of Regulations 20.4.2, 20.4.3 and 20.4.5 shall apply.

SPECIAL EVENTS/EVENTS OF CLASSES/ISAF EVENTS

20.6 Category C applies.

20.6.1 ISAF shall administer an Event Advertising System and/or Individual Advertising System for boats participating in the following events:

(i) **Special Events**
America's Cup Match and Challenger/Defender Series

Volvo Ocean Race
Global Ocean Races
Trans-Oceanic Races
IMS World Championships
Professional Windsurfers Association Events (PWA)
FICO Lacoste World Championship

(ii) **Events of Classes**
International America's Cup Class
Volvo 60'
Maxi One Design
Open 60 Monohull Class (incorporates Open 50 Class)
Open 60 Multihull Class
PWA Classes
49'er Grand Prix series

(iii) Proposals for other Special Events and/or class events of equal or similar status may, on the initiative of the Executive Committee or on application by an event *organizing authority* (with the approval of the relevant National Authority) be put to the Executive Committee for approval. This approval shall be reported to the next Council Meeting.

(iv) **ISAF Events**
ISAF Youth Sailing World Championship
ISAF Sailing World Championships
ISAF Offshore Team World Championship
ISAF World Sailing Games
ISAF Match Racing World Championship
ISAF Women's Match Racing World Championship
ISAF Team Racing World Championship
ISAF Women's Keelboat World Championship

.. and any other ISAF Events which may be introduced.

FEES

20.7 All boats carrying Category C advertising in line with Regulations 20.4 to 20.5.1 may be required to pay a fee only to their National Authority (no share to ISAF or any other National Authorities).

20.7.1 All Events under Regulation 20.6.1 carrying Category C advertising shall pay a fee to ISAF.

ENTRY FEES

20.8 There shall be no variation of entry fees based on the *competitor's* category of advertising for the boat in which he is competing.

PROTESTS UNDER THIS CODE

20.9 When, after finding the facts, a protest committee decides that a boat or her crew has broken a section of this Code, it shall:

(a) give a warning; or

(b) disqualify the boat in accordance with RRS 64.1; or

(c) disqualify the boat from more than one race or from the series when it decides that the breach warrants a stronger penalty; or

(d) act under RRS 69.1 when it decides that there may have been a gross breach.

DEFINITIONS

20.10 The following definitions shall apply to this Code only:

Note: *There are some definitions which are not needed in the present text of the Code.*

(a) **All Classes**
Shall include all Classes as defined below and shall include Classes which are designated as ISAF Classes as well as Classes which are not designated as ISAF Classes;

(b) **Class**
A Class of boat/sailboard includes boats/sailboards which conform to a physical specification intended to allow competitive racing among the Class, and without limiting the generality of the foregoing, includes Classes with one-design, restricted, and developmental specifications as these terms are applied generally and for which there is an existing organization to administer the Class which has:

(i) an Executive or similar body which administers the Class;

(ii) a membership which is open to all owners of boats/sailboards which meet the specification of the Class; and

(iii) which holds a meeting of members at least once a year, and which gives notice of such meetings to all members;

(c) **National Class**
A National Class for the purposes of this Regulation is a class where the National Authority has substantial authority in the direction or management of the Class;

(d) **Club or Invitational Event**
A Club event is an event that is sponsored, organized or held by a Club which has sailing as one of its activities.

An Invitational event is one in which the participants are invited and is not open to members of a participating class except by invitation.

(e) **Hull Length**
For the purposes of this Regulation, Hull Length is as defined in the applicable Class rules for Hull Length or any comparable measurement less Hull Appendages and if no means of measurement exists in the Class rules, Hull Length and Hull Appendage shall have the meaning set out in the Equipment Rules of Sailing, D.3.1 and E.1.1;

(f) **Organizing Authority**
Shall have the definition contained in RRS 87.1;

(g) **Competitor**
In addition to its natural meaning, a competitor in respect of any boat shall include any person who has the right to use the boat as owner or by charter, loan or otherwise;

(h) **Competitor Advertising**
In respect of any boat is advertising which is applied to a boat, its equipment or the person or the equipment of a competitor or competitors as the condition of or as the result of a payment made to or made as a result of the direction of one or more of the competitors in respect of such boat;

(i) **Other Advertising**
Advertising which is not competitor advertising;

(j) **Bow Number**
An identifier assigned to a boat, usually for the duration of an event, by the organizer which is required to be displayed on the bow of a boat which may be a combination of numbers and letters.

REGULATION 21
ANTI-DOPING CODE

See rule 5.

NOTE: ISAF have accepted the World Anti-Doping Code (the *'Code'*). This regulation implements the *'Code'* in the sport of sailing. The regulation is available on the ISAF website and is about 30 A4 pages in length.

PRESCRIPTIONS

The RYA Prescribes

Rule

50.4 Headsails

Rule 50.4 shall not apply. A spinnaker is defined as a sail set forward of the foremost mast with half width (measured as a spinnaker) greater than 75% of foot. Any other sail tacked down forward of the foremost mast is a headsail. The terms and definitions used by this prescription shall be as in the *Equipment Rules of Sailing.*

68 Damages

1. Any claim for damages arising from an incident while a boat is bound by the Racing Rules of Sailing shall be subject to the jurisdiction of the courts and not considered by a protest committee.
2. A boat that takes a penalty or retires does not thereby admit liability for damages or that she has broken a rule.

70.4 Right of Appeal

RYA approval is not required to deny the right of appeal under rule 70.4(a). However, the denial of appeal shall not apply

1. when it was not essential to determine promptly the result of a race or series, or
2. to a party to a hearing under rule 69.1, Allegations of Gross Misconduct, but the decision of the protest committee shall determine the results of the event.

78 Compliance with Class Rules; Certificates

The race committee may inspect or measure any boat, as defined in the *Equipment Rules of Sailing* C.2.1, or personal equipment, as defined in the *Equipment Rules of Sailing* C.1.3, at any time.

86.3 Rule Changes

An organizing authority wishing to develop and test a rule change may do so but shall obtain prior approval from and report the results to the RYA.

87 Changes To National Authority Prescriptions

Notices of race and sailing instructions shall not change a prescription of the RYA, other than the prescriptions to rules 50.4, 78 and Appendix G.

APPENDIX F APPEALS PROCEDURES

F2.1 Submission of Documents

Rule F2.1 shall not apply. Instead, within 15 days of receiving the protest committee's written decision or its decision not to reopen a hearing, the appellant shall notify RYA Racing stating an intention to lodge an appeal. No details are needed at this stage. The RYA will send the appellant an Appeal Form, which shall be completed as far as possible, to form the appeal, and returned to the RYA within 15 days together with a copy of the protest committee's decision. The appeal shall state why the appellant believes the protest committee's decision or its procedures were incorrect.

If the appellant fails to meet the requirements of the appeals procedure the RYA will refuse to hear the appeal save in exceptional circumstances. If other parties to the protest or the protest committee fail to meet the requirements of the procedure the RYA may decide the appeal as it thinks fit.

F4 Comments

The national authority may additionally invite comments from boats and other organizations that are not parties to the hearing.

APPENDIX G IDENTIFICATION ON SAILS

G1 Identification

The requirements of rules G1.1, G1.2 and G1.3 apply to all British owned boats except that:

(a) under rule G1.1(a), class insignia need not be carried when the boat carries a sail number from one of the series specified in G2(a), (b), (c) or (d) below.

(b) under rule G1.1(c), a sail number of more than four digits may be carried.

(c) under rule G1.1(c), for boats other than ISAF classes, one of the authorities specified in G2 below shall allot an appropriate sail number.

(d) under rule G1.2(b), the height of a letter included as part of a sail number shall be the same as any numerals included in the sail number.

(e) under rule G1.3(c), the national letters may be placed in front of or above the sail numbers.

G2 Series of sail numbers and issuing authorities approved by the RYA

(a) Y,M,N,T,A and L series issued by the RYA.

(b) R series issued by the Royal Ocean Racing Club.

(c) C series issued by the Clyde Yacht Clubs Association.

(d) National class series issued by the RYA.

(e) Series issued by RYA affiliated class associations and approved by the RYA.

(f) Series issued by a builder of a new class and approved by the RYA.

REGULATION 20, ADVERTISING CODE

Regulation 20.4.2

When the display of Category C advertising is permitted, UK competitors are licensed to display the advertising, and no individual application to the RYA is needed.

Regulation 20.4.3

An organizing authority wishing to restrict advertising in an event to Category A shall apply to the RYA at least 15 days before publishing the notice of race, confirming:

(a) for a club event, that the event:

- (i) is sponsored, organized or held by a club which has sailing as one of its activities, and
- (ii) does not form part of a wider series for which Category C boats are eligible, and
- (iii) is not a qualifier for another event for which Category C boats are eligible.

(b) for an invitational event, that the event is not a qualifier for an International Class event.

The RYA will normally grant approval if such an application is received. The restriction to Category A and the RYA statement of approval shall be included in the notice of race. Any restriction to Category A shall apply to boats while they are racing. When the organizing authority wishes the restriction to apply at other times during an event, it shall specify such times, and the reasons, in its initial application. If this extra restriction is approved by the RYA, it and the RYA statement of approval shall be included in the notice of race.

Regulation 20.4.4

The RYA Technical Unit can advise on standard wording for restrictions to Category C to be included in class rules.

Regulation 20.5

(a) A controller of a handicap system or rating rule may request the RYA:

(i) to decide that races held under that system or rule are Category C, or are Category C with restrictions stated in the request.

(ii) to sub-divide the system or rule into two or more sub-systems or sub-rules with different Categories. Race results may later be combined.

The RYA will normally agree to such a request.

(b) For races for which scoring under the RYA Portsmouth Yardstick Scheme is specified, the advertising category (for UK competitors under ISAF regulation 20.5) will be Category C.

(c) When a handicap system is controlled by the organizing authority for the races to be sailed under that system and when permission as required has been received from the RYA for Category C advertising to be displayed, the notice of race shall so state, and shall state any approved restriction.

(d) Regulation 20.4.3, and the prescription thereto, apply to clubs organising handicap racing.

Regulation 20.7

Boats displaying Category C advertising are not required to pay a fee to the RYA.

RYA

GUIDANCE NOTES

The RYA publishes guidance notes on its website to help competitors, race organizers and race officials. The following guidance notes are available at August 2004; additional guidance notes will be published as required. Please note that the guidance offered is the opinion of experts and is not a binding interpretation of the rules.

The latest versions of these guidance notes can be obtained from the RYA website www.rya.org.uk/racing/rules.asp.

Comments or questions are welcome and should be made by email to the RYA at racing@rya.org.uk.

Main Changes to the Racing Rules

This explains the main changes made to the Racing Rules of Sailing 2005-2008 (RRS) compared with the previous version.

Notices of Race and Sailing Instructions

This explains the changes required to notices of race and sailing instructions consequent on the changes in the RRS 2005-2008.

Rule 69 – Allegations of Gross Misconduct

There are two guidance notes concerning bad behaviour in the sport of sailing. The first, which is also printed on the next two pages, is directed mainly at competitors. The second is a detailed set of questions and answers to guide protest committees on how to deal with alleged bad behaviour. This guidance includes how and when to initiate a hearing and sets out the correct procedures for a protest committee to ensure that an allegation against a competitor is fairly heard and considered.

Appendix A – Scoring

This contains a detailed review of the scoring rules with recommendations for sailing instructions, race committee procedures and scoring calculations complete with examples.

ISAF Regulation 20 – Advertising Code

This contains important information for race organizers and class associations and explains the application of the RYA prescription to the regulation.

RYA

GUIDANCE ON RULE 69

Rule 69 is used by the sport of sailboat racing to control and penalize unacceptable behaviour during an event. It covers on and off-the-water behaviour. Action under rule 69 is entirely separate from any protest and any resulting penalty arising from any other rule that may have been broken.

The protest committee may receive reports from competitors, officials or spectators, or may initiate action of its own accord. It may decide merely to interview the competitor, or to act under rule 69.1. If proceeding with a rule 69.1 hearing, the protest committee must promptly inform the competitor in writing of the alleged misconduct.

Allegations have to be proven beyond reasonable doubt under rule 69.1. Competitors are entitled to be accompanied by a friend, coach or parent or other advisor at the hearing.

If the protest committee decides that the competitor did commit the alleged misconduct, it may issue a warning, or it may penalize the competitor or the boat. If it does penalize, it reports this penalty to the RYA which, when appropriate, may impose further penalty beyond the jurisdiction of the protest committee.

The following levels of action are among those available to protest committees following receipt of a rule 69 report (levels 1 to 5 following a hearing):

- Interview with competitor, but no hearing and so no penalty is possible (level 0)
- Warning but no penalty (level 1)
- Increase the boat's points score (level 2)
- Exclude competitor and, when appropriate, disqualify the boat:
    - from one or more races (level 3)
    - from the event (level 4)
    - from event and recommend further action by RYA (level 5).

The table overleaf shows types of alleged behaviour that will lead to a rule 69 hearing, and the appropriate outcome if the allegation is proven. The range of outcomes allows the seriousness of the offence, whether it is a repeated offence and the attitude of the competitor to be taken into account.

Behaviour	Outcome
A breach of a racing rule that may be sufficiently serious, or linked to unacceptable behaviour, such that the normal penalty may be inadequate	1 – 4
Repeating the same measurement offence with intent	3 – 5
Bullying, intimidating, or discriminatory behaviour against another competitor	3 – 5
Lying in a protest committee hearing	3 – 5
Foul language: intended to offend, or inappropriate for the occasion or location	1 – 4
Fighting and assaults	3 – 5
Intentionally disobeying a reasonable request of the organizing authority or its officials	1 – 5
Abuse of officials	1 – 5
Theft, or damage or abuse of property	3 – 5

Full guidance notes on conduct of rule 69 hearings may be downloaded from www.rya.org.uk/racing/rules.asp

TIME AND SPEED CHARTS

Time in seconds to advance 1 length

Boat Speed Knots	Length of Yacht in Metres						
	4	5	6	7	8	9	10
1	7.8	9.7	11.7	13.6	15.5	17.5	19.4
2	3.9	4.9	5.8	6.8	7.8	8.7	9.7
3	2.6	3.2	3.9	4.5	5.2	5.8	6.5
4	1.9	2.4	2.9	3.4	3.9	4.4	4.9
5	1.6	1.9	2.3	2.7	3.1	3.5	3.9
6	1.3	1.6	1.9	2.3	2.6	2.9	3.2
7	1.1	1.4	1.7	1.9	2.2	2.5	2.8
8	1.0	1.2	1.5	1.7	1.9	2.2	2.4
9	0.9	1.1	1.3	1.5	1.7	1.9	2.2
10	0.8	1.0	1.2	1.4	1.6	1.7	1.9

1 knot = 0.515 m/sec = 1.666ft/sec

Boat velocities for given wind speeds

This table gives approximations only. Velocities are for non-planing boats that are reaching or running. For beating, velocities will be lower and multiplying by 0.8 will yield an approximate result.

Wind		Waterline length of boat in metres													
		3		4		5		6		7		8		9	
Kn	Bft	Kn	m/sec	Kn	m/sec	Kn	m/sec	Kn	m/sec	Kn	m/sec	Kn	m/sec	Kn	m/sec
1	1	0.2	0.1	0.2	0.1	0.2	0.1	0.2	0.1	0.3	0.1	0.3	0.1	0.4	0.2
2		0.4	0.2	0.5	0.2	0.4	0.2	0.4	0.2	0.5	0.3	0.7	0.3	0.8	0.4
3		0.7	0.4	0.6	0.3	0.7	0.4	0.7	0.3	0.8	0.4	1.0	0.5	1.2	0.6
4	2	0.9	0.5	0.9	0.5	0.9	0.5	0.9	0.5	1.1	0.6	1.3	0.7	1.6	0.8
5		1.1	0.6	1.1	0.6	1.1	0.6	1.1	0.6	1.4	0.7	1.7	0.9	2.0	1.0
6		1.4	0.7	1.4	0.7	1.4	0.7	1.4	0.7	1.7	0.9	2.1	1.1	2.4	1.3
7	3	1.6	0.8	1.6	0.8	1.6	0.8	1.6	0.8	2.0	1.0	2.4	1.2	2.8	1.5
11	4	2.5	1.3	2.6	1.3	2.6	1.3	2.6	1.3	3.1	1.6	3.8	2.0	4.5	2.3
17	5	4.0	2.0	3.9	2.0	4.0	2.1	4.1	2.1	4.9	2.5	5.9	3.0	6.9	3.6
22	6	5.2	2.7	5.1	2.6	5.1	2.6	5.3	2.7	6.3	3.2	7.7	4.0	9.0	4.7

1 metre = 3.281 feet

BEAUFORT SCALE

Wind Bft	Kn	Km/hr	m/sec	ft/sec	
1	1	1.85	0.51	1.69	Light air, ripples
	2	3.71	103	3.38	
	3	5.56	1.54	5.07	
2	4	7.41	2.06	6.76	Light breeze, small wavelets
	5	9.27	2.57	8.44	
	6	11.12	3.09	10.13	
3	7	12.97	3.60	11.82	Gentle breeze, large wavelets
	8	14.82	4.12	13.51	
	9	16.68	4.63	15.20	
	10	18.53	5.15	16.89	
4	11	20.38	5.66	18.58	Moderate breeze, small waves, frequent white horses
	12	22.24	6.18	20.27	
	13	24.09	6.69	21.96	
	14	25.94	7.21	23.64	
	15	27.80	7.72	25.33	
	16	29.65	8.24	27.02	
5	17	31.50	8.75	28.71	Fresh breeze, moderate waves, white horses.
	18	33.36	9.27	30.40	
	19	35.21	9.78	32.09	
	20	37.06	10.29	33.78	
	21	38.91	10.81	35.47	
6	22	40.77	11.32	37.16	Strong breeze, foaming crests
	23	42.62	11.84	38.84	
	24	44.47	12.35	40.53	
	25	46.33	12.87	42.22	

INDEX

References are to rule numbers (for example, 27.3), appendices and their rule numbers (for example, C or E3.10), and sections of the book (for example, Introduction, Race Signals). Italics indicate words that appear in Definitions. Appendices K, L and M are not indexed except for their titles.

INDEX

RACE SIGNALS

The meanings of visual and sound signals are stated below. An arrow pointing up or down (↑ ↓) means that a visual signal is displayed or removed. A dot (●) means a sound; five short dashes (– – – – –) mean repetitive sounds. A long dash (——) means a long sound. When a visual signal is displayed over a class flag, the signal applies only to that class.

POSTPONEMENT SIGNALS

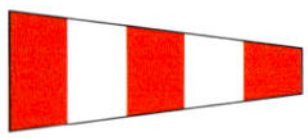

↑ ●●

↓ ●

AP

Races not started are *postponed*. The warning signal will be made 1 minute after removal unless at that time the race is *postponed* again or *abandoned*.

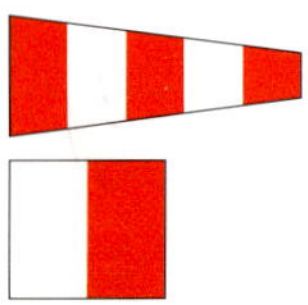

↑ ●●

AP over H

Races not started are *postponed*. Further signals ashore.

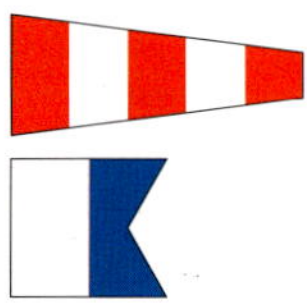

↑ ●●

AP over A

Races not started are *postponed*.
No more racing today.

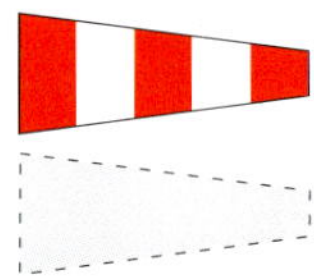

↑ ●●

↓ ●

AP over a numeral pennant

Hours *postponement* from the scheduled starting time.

ABANDONMENT SIGNALS

↑ ●●●

↓ ●

N

All races that have started are *abandoned*. Return to the starting area. The warning signal will be made 1 minute after removal unless at that time the race is *abandoned* again or *postponed.*

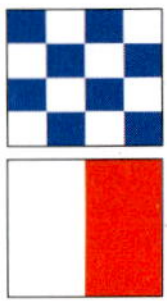

↑ ●●●

N over H

All races are *abandoned*.
Further signals ashore.

↑ ●●●

N over A

All races are *abandoned*.
No more racing today.